Grammar Dimensions

Workbook Three

Grammar Dimensions
Workbook Three

Kathleen Flynn
Glendale College

Heinle & Heinle Publishers

I⟨T⟩P **An International Thomson Publishing Company**

Boston, Massachusetts 02116 U.S.A.

Photos on: page 35, courtesy of the Louisiana Office of Tourism; page 55, courtesy of Pat Martin.

Contents

Grammar Dimensions

Workbook Three

UNIT

1 Overview of the English Verb System
Time and Tense

(Focus 1)

Select the appropriate form of each verb in parentheses.

Robert **(1)** _____ (be) really worried. Right now, most students **(2)** _____ (register) for their fall courses, but he **(3)** _____ (can [negative]). The computer **(4)** _____ (say) that Robert **(5)** _____ (owe) the college $6,000 for last semester. He **(6)** _____ (know) that his father **(7)** _____ (pay) that tuition bill last year!

What **(8)** _____ (shall) Robert do? The registrar **(9)** _____ (ask) for a copy of the canceled tuition check. Robert **(10)** _____ (call) his father later tonight. He **(11)** _____ (hope) that his father **(12)** _____ (keep) good records.

EXERCISE 2 **(Focus 1)**

Name the time frame (present, past, or future) of each verb in Exercise 1.

1. _____

2. _____

3. _____

4. _____

5. _____

6. _____

7. _____

8. _____

9. _____

10. _____

11. _____

12. _____

EXERCISE 3   (Focus 2)

Select the appropriate form of each verb in parentheses.

Scientists **(1)** _____ (discover) that being left-handed is linked to death at earlier age. A psychologist at the University of California at San Bernardino **(2)** _____ (test) people who **(3)** _____ (switch) from being left-handed to being right-handed, as well as those who **(4)** _____ (remain) left-handed. Both groups **(5)** _____ (die) at an earlier age than the general population.

One way to explain this result **(6)** _____ (be) that most electrical machinery is built for right-handed people. Accidents **(7)** _____ (occur) when this equipment is used by "lefties."

The scientists **(8)** _____ (recommend [negative]) forcing children to become right-handed. Instead, their report **(9)** _____ (focus) on the special needs of left-handed people and how society **(10)** _____ (change, already) to accommodate those needs.

EXERCISE 4   (Focus 2)

Name the tense (form) of each verb in Exercise 3.

1. _____   7. _____

2. _____   8. _____

3. _____   9. _____

4. _____   10. _____

5. _____   11. _____

6. _____   12. _____

EXERCISE 5 (Focus 3)

Mark each of the following passages with a slash (/) to show where the time frame changes. The first one has been done for you.

1. I'm always happy when winter is over. / Last year I fell on some ice and hurt my hip. I went to the hospital for X rays and had to remain in bed for a week. / Now my hip hurts whenever it rains.

2. Every day people are discovering new uses for old materials. Just yesterday I read a story about using old tire tubes for floating down the river. The story said that the old tubes could be used for a year or more. What will they think of next?

3. For more than 30 years, Dr. Simmons has been curing patients in the office on the first floor of his home. He has mended broken bones and delivered babies in this office. Recently, however, the county medical association has ordered him to move his office to a separate building. The association insists that the old office doesn't meet modern standards. Dr. Simmons will probably retire and close his medical practice rather than go through an expensive move. What a loss for the community!

4. I was happy when I opened my mailbox yesterday. The mail contained a letter from my family and my tax refund check. What will I do with the money? First, I need to repair my car. Then I will hire someone to paint my living room. I really don't like to paint.

EXERCISE 6 (Focus 3)

Identify and underline the moment of focus in the following passages. There may be more than one, and sometimes it will be implied. The first one has been done for you.

1. <u>When the accident occurred</u>, Paul's mind was not on his driving. He had been thinking about his upcoming vacation and all the fishing and sailing that he was going to do. <u>By the time that the police arrived</u>, however, he was fully aware of the damage that had resulted from the accident.

2. In the future, a computerized scanner in your refrigerator will keep track of the groceries that you need. The computer will either print out the list of groceries or it will contact the computer at the grocery store and place your weekly order.

3. On January 1, much of the world will celebrate New Year's Day. People will yell "Happy New Year!" and then drink a toast to good fortune and happiness in the coming year.

4. The ancient Greeks built many marble temples to their gods. These temples were often situated in high places so that they could be seen from a distance and would be close to the gods.

5. The first person walked on the moon in 1969. This historic event was seen on television all over the world.

6. Paul Gauguin was a banker in Paris who was completely bored with his life and work. Shortly after he turned 40, Gauguin left Paris for Tahiti. There he painted pictures of Tahitian women. These paintings can be seen today in museums and private collections.

7. The mathematical concept of "zero" was first conceived of in Ancient India. The concept was later accepted in other countries.

8. Right now, Kate is studying a combined major—business and health care. As soon as she completes 36 units of her major, she will be eligible for a workstudy program. Then she will work in a small hospital and take classes at the same time.

9. For more than five years, David has been a resident doctor in a pediatric surgery program at Atwater Hospital. He spends most of his days and nights performing surgery on young children. He must also explain the need for this surgery to their parents.

10. Melinda had three different vaccinations before she left for her research work overseas. Her arm was sore for several days afterward.

UNIT

2 Overview of the English Verb System

Aspect

EXERCISE 1   *(Focus 1)*

Circle the meaning of the aspect of the highlighted verb.

EXAMPLE: Tom **has been collecting** stamps since he was 10 years old.
  a. He no longer collects them.
  b. He still collects them.

1. Janet **is storing** some of her furniture at her parents' house until her new house is ready.
  a. This is temporary.
  b. This is permanent.

2. The student **interrupted** the professor's lecture to clarify a point.
  a. This happened just once.
  b. This happens repeatedly.

3. Charles **sings** in the student choir every week.
  a. He is doing this right now.
  b. He does this on a regular basis.

4. Anna **has been trying** to finish her term paper for over a week.
  a. The term paper is complete.
  b. The term paper is unfinished.

5. Teachers **wear** chalk on their clothes.
  a. They usually do this.
  b. They have been doing this recently because it is stylish.

DUANE GILLOGLY

EXERCISE 2 (Focuses 2 and 3)

Decide whether to use the simple or the progressive aspect of each verb in parentheses in the following sentences.

1. The duplicating machine _____ (keep) making handouts for the instructors.

2. The postal carrier _____ (deliver) the mail when the dog _____ (attack).

3. Last night, I _____ (take) the wrong bus.

4. Dr. Traugott _____ (speak) six languages fluently.

5. Janice _____ (decide, still) where to live.

6. Wilson _____ (watch) TV everyday.

7. Yesterday, the governor _____ (propose) a change in the tax laws.

8. I _____ (remember) her name after she _____ (walk) away.

9. It _____ (snow) a lot in Siberia.

10. It's _____ (snow) right now in many parts of the world.

EXERCISE 3 (Focus 4)

Decide whether to use the perfect or the simple aspect of each verb in parentheses in the following sentences.

1. The professor _____ (grade) three reports so far this semester.

2. The judge who ruled in several landmark cases _____ (die) yesterday of natural causes.

3. Louise, a French major, _____ (visit) France three times and will go back again this summer.

4. I _____ (live) in Ohio for a year before moving to New York.

5. Before Janet started this job, she _____ (work, never) before.

6. My grandfather _____ (immigrate) from Germany to the United States as a young man.

7. Before that, he _____ (travel, only) for his work.

8. His work as a carpenter's apprentice _____ (take) him from Germany to Alsace-Lorraine, which is now part of France.

9. His granddaughter now _____ (fly) across the Atlantic as part of her work.

10. She travels so much that she _____ (be) around the world twice.

EXERCISE 4   (Focus 4)

Discuss with other students in class the differences in meaning between the simple and perfect aspects of the verbs in the following sentence pairs.

1. The actor practiced his part for days.
   The actor has practiced that part before.

2. I did my share of housecleaning this weekend.
   I've been doing my share of the housecleaning.

3. The government didn't change the law regarding indoor smoking.
   The government hasn't changed the indoor smoking law yet.

4. Bob has started a new business several times.
   Bob started a new business last week.

5. Carl cooked dinner last night.
   Carl has cooked dinner since he left home.

EXERCISE 5   (Focus 5)

Decide whether to use the perfect or the perfect progressive aspect of each verb in parentheses in the following sentences. More than one answer may be correct.

1. The professor _____ (lecture) for more than an hour before the class requested a break.

2. I _____ (eat) at that restaurant several times. I recommend it.

3. Nancy _____ (try) to reach the gas company all afternoon, but the line _____ (is) busy.

4. The university _____ (increase) tuition twice in the past three years.

5. NASA scientists _____ (search) for a better method to detect engine problems since the *Challenger* disaster.

6. Medical, law, and business schools _____ (change) their admissions policies regarding women and minorities.

7. That restaurant _____ (stop) accepting checks.

8. By next march, Josefina _____ (live) in the United States for seven years.

9. Even though it's spring vacation, Tom _____ (write) his term paper all week.

10. I _____ (study) English since I arrived in the United States.

Aspect   **7**

EXERCISE 6 (General Review)

Write the appropriate form of each verb in parentheses in the following paragraphs.

Ballooning!

Noriko and her friends **(1)** _____ (plan) to go ballooning for months.
She first **(2)** _____ (learn) about this sport from a TV program. Since then, she
(3) _____ (rent) videos about ballooning to learn more about it. She
(4) _____ (convince) her friends to go on a trip with her. They
(5) _____ (decide) to go after they **(6)** _____ (finish) the
semester.

They **(7)** _____ (select, already) the balloon rental company. They
(8) _____ (meet) with the owner and **(9)** _____ (make)
transportation and camping arrangements. Since they **(10)** _____ (can
[negative]) sleep in the balloon, they **(11)** _____ (need) tents and camping
equipment. All of them **(12)** _____ (look) forward to their adventure in the sky.

EXERCISE 7 (General Review)

**Discuss with other students the differences in meaning among the following two or
three sentences.**

1. John smoked for five years.
   John has smoked for five years.
   John smokes.

2. They're studying.
   They've been studying.
   They study.

3. She's eating in the cafeteria.
   She's been eating in the cafeteria.
   She ate in the cafeteria.

4. Tina tried to cash her check at the bank.
   Tina has been trying to cash this check for two days.

5. I have been driving for several years.
   I drove in Europe.

6. Mark drinks milk.
   Mark has been drinking milk ever since his ulcer was diagnosed.

7. Mr. Warner has worked for IBM for 35 years.
   Mr. Warner worked for IBM for 35 years.

8. Eric paints.
   Eric is painting right now.

9. Dr. Lang performed surgery at 9:45 P.M.
   Dr. Lang has performed surgery on that patient before.

10. Catherine answers the phone in the Dean's Office.
    Catherine had answered the phone in the emergency clinic.

UNIT

3 Adverbial Phrases and Clauses

EXERCISE 1 *(Focus 1)*

Complete each sentence below with an adverbial. First read each sentence carefully to determine the meaning of what is being asked or stated. If you need help, refer to pages 29 to 31 of your textbook.

1. _____ will you spend on your next vacation?

2. _____ will you spend your next vacation?

3. _____ have you been living in this city?

4. I'll do the wash _____ I have time.

5. _____ does Rita manage to afford such an expensive car?

6. _____ did Gloria return to her country so suddenly?

7. _____ do you visit your family?

8. _____ did Jack dress for his interview?

9. The professor asked _____ each student had spent on the term project.

10. _____ I had the chance, I spoke to Madeline about the assignment.

Underline the adverbials in each sentence and then label each. Follow the example.

EXAMPLE: Kate <u>always</u> objects <u>strenuously</u> <u>when</u> someone <u>at work</u> forgets
          frequency   manner time   place
    <u>to turn on the fax machine.</u>
          purpose

1. Usually companies have rules regarding where and when workers can eat in the office.

2. At Argus Word Processing, employees may only eat in the kitchen area and only at lunch time or on breaks.

3. Ms. Lionetti vigorously enforces this rule to keep the office machines clean.

4. Once I heard her explain how a spilled cup of coffee ruined a piece of equipment in the fax area.

5. She replaced the machine right away.

6. The next day, there were signs on all the walls that clearly explained the new policy.

7. Food and drinks could only be had in the kitchen area and only at specified times to reduce accidents.

8. In the past, typists had often gotten food stains on the manuscript pages.

9. Now, the pages are always clean because no food is allowed near the office equipment.

10. These days Ms. Lionetti often complains that no one has remembered to make coffee.

Add the adverbials in parentheses to each sentence. More than one position may be possible.

EXAMPLE: Jack doesn't get to class.   (sometimes)   (on time)

Sometimes Jack doesn't get to class on time.

Jack sometimes doesn't get to class on time.

1. Belinda goes to the Bahamas. (every winter) (to make sure she gets a tan)

   _____

   _____

2. She swims two miles. (in order to keep in shape) (every day) (in the ocean)

   _____

   _____

3. Belinda applies sunscreen. (whenever she can) (to her body)

   _____

   _____

4. She eats fruit and fish. (because they are fresh) (every day)

   _____

   _____

5. She stopped eating meat and chicken. (recently) (to lose weight)

   _____

   _____

6. She will continue to eat. (when she goes home) (carefully)

   _____

   _____

Describe a custom or tradition in your country that must be done:

1. carefully
2. every year
3. outdoors
4. before marriage
5. occasionally
6. before eating
7. after sundown
8. alone
9. every week
10. with your family

EXERCISE 5   (*Focus 3*)

With a partner, examine the following sentences. Write a "C" for those that are correct. Rewrite the sentences that are incorrect. Discuss why you changed the position or order of an adverbial phrase.

1. Jerry eats out on a regular basis in local restaurants.

_____

_____

2. He discovered recently a Thai restaurant in Hollywood in his neighborhood.

_____

_____

3. He invited several friends to meet him for dinner.

_____

_____

4. He will meet them tonight in the lobby at 7 P.M.

_____

_____

5. Unfortunately, he gave them the wrong directions due to some confusion to the restaurant.

_____

_____

6. Right now, his friends are looking for 4021 Hollywood Boulevard instead of 4201.

_____

_____

7. He's hoping as if his life depended on it sincerely that they look in a phone book for the correct address.

_____

_____

EXERCISE 6 (Focus 5)

Determine whether the order of the main clause and the adverbial clause are correct or whether the sentence should be rewritten. Mark the sentence with a "C" or rewrite the incorrect sentences. Pay attention to the meaning of each clause.

1. So that he could afford to pay his car insurance, Benjamin took on a second job.

_____

_____

2. Ever since he first tried skydiving, Martin has been in love with the sport.

_____

_____

3. After he died, the old man entered the hospital.

_____

_____

4. Where the truck drivers eat, I eat.

_____

_____

5. As soon as I bought the house, I began to have second thoughts.

_____

_____

6. First he waxed the car, then he washed it.

_____

_____

7. Whenever I smell fresh bread, I remember my grandmother's kitchen.

_____

_____

8. So that she could spend more time using computers, Sally got a job in the computer lab.

_____

_____

9. As if it were nothing, Jane wrote with both hands at the same time.

_____

_____

10. Because many people steal clothing from stores, store owners now put tags with permanent dye on their expensive clothing and coats.

_____

_____

UNIT

4 Passive Verbs

EXERCISE 1 (*Focus 1*)

Decide on the correct passive form of each verb in parentheses in the following sentences. Look closely at the highlighted time expressions; they are clues to the needed time frame of the passive voice.

Every day, a lot of things go on in class—papers **(1)** _____ (hand) out, homework **(2)** _____ (collect), and assignments **(3)** _____ given). **Yesterday,** a video **(4)** _____ (show) in theater class. The day before, the same story **(5)** _____ (perform) on stage.

Right now, the video **(6)** _____ (compare) to the live performance. My class partner is writing down comments so that by tomorrow the assignment **(7)** _____ (can, complete). The assignment **(8)** _____ (grade) next week. The two students with the highest scores **(9)** _____ (excuse [future]) from taking the final. I hope we **(10)** _____ (select).

EXERCISE 2 (*Focus 1*)

Ben works in his school's Financial Aid Office. In this exercise he describes a number of activities that take place there. Decide on the correct form of the passive voice for each verb in parentheses. Look closely at the highlighted time expressions in each sentence.

Financial Aid may sound boring to you, but **every day** hundreds of applications **(1)** _____ (process) by this office. Loans and grants **(2)** _____ (give out) **each week** and more loans and grants **(3)** _____ (apply for) by new students. **On almost any day,** a student **(4)** _____ (give) money or **(5)** _____ (tell) to apply for a different type of grant.

Applications need to **(6)** _____ (fill out) carefully. **Yesterday,** a student **(7)** _____ (turn down) for financial aid because his form **(8)** _____ (complete [negative]) correctly. **Last year's** income

16   Unit 4

(9) _____ (write) in the space for this year's salary. Oh, well, the form will have to **(10)** _____ (redo). When you need help with financial aid forms, drop in and see me. I'll help you do it right the first time.

EXERCISE 3 (Focus 1)

Underline all the verbs in the following paragraph. Then, if a form is not correct, cross it out and write the correct form above it. Follow the examples.

How Coffee Beans Are Processed

First, the beans <u>are picked</u> by hand. Then they ~~send~~ ^{are sent} to the factory ~~to roast~~ ^{to be roasted}. Sometimes the coffee beans age before they have been roasted. Americans, Germans, and Scandinavians prefer dark roasted beans. Light roasted beans prefer for blending. Coffee beans from Kenya and Ethiopia are used both for blending and for their own flavors.

After the beans have roasted, they cool and the batch is being tested. If the batch is good, the beans are placed in bags, sell, and shipped to market.

Using the information provided, write a story on the processing of orange juice. Follow the example.

First	oranges	pick, clean
Then	oranges	cut
	juice	squeeze out

Orange skins		throw away
		or
		use for fertilizer

Next,	most of the liquid	take out
Result	juice	concentrate
Then,	juice	freeze
	and	
	juice	ship to market
Last step	water add	customer	to make juice

EXAMPLE:

First the oranges are picked and cleaned. Then they are cut and the juice squeezed out.

_____

_____

_____

_____

_____

EXERCISE 5   (Focus 1)

Describe some other foods or products that are made in your country. Some sample products and the verbs that are associated with them are provided for you.

Wine: grapes—selected, picked, washed, crushed
wine—aged, bottled, selected, sold, served

Cheese: milk—aged, cooked, stored
cheese—sliced, grated, aged, flavored, processed, sold

Suit: cloth—selected, cut, sewn, fitted
suit—tried on, altered, pressed, sold

Book: idea—developed, accepted, written, edited, revised
pages—printed, illustrated

Airplane: design—specified, drawn, changed, accepted
plane—built, tested, flown, sold

EXERCISE 6 (Focus 2)

Underline the passive constructions in the following paragraphs. For each passive that you can find, mark the verb's receiver with "R." If an agent is mentioned, indicate it with "A." The first sentence has been done as an example.

R   A

(1) Many UFOs or unidentified flying objects <u>have been reported</u> by people all over the world. **(2)** They are most often sighted in isolated areas—farms, swamps, and fields. **(3)** UFOs are usually described as round or "saucerlike." **(4)** That is why they have been nicknamed "flying saucers."

(5) A few years ago, a flying saucer was reported by a man in a small town in Georgia. **(6)** According to the newspaper account, the man was followed by the UFO for more than 20 minutes. **(7)** He claimed that a strange light was given off by the UFO. **(8)** Lights on flying saucers have been reported by others as well. **(9)** It seems that the lights are a form of communication. **(10)** Some people have claimed that they have been abducted by these lighted ships. **(11)** Once on board the UFO, they were examined with instruments that they had never seen before.

(12) Are these stories fact or fiction? **(13)** No one really knows, but one thing is certain. **(14)** Flying saucers have been a popular topic in newspapers and movies for years.

EXERCISE 7 (Focus 3)

Underline the _by_ phrase in each of the following sentences and then decide whether it is necessary. If it's not, cross it out.

> EXAMPLE: Millions of birthday cards are sent ~~by people~~ every year.
>
> The Polaroid camera was invented <u>by Edwin Land</u>.

1. That book was translated by the translator.
2. More and more murders are being committed by women.
3. I was given a speeding ticket by a police officer.
4. That surgery was performed by a surgeon at 6 A.M. this morning.
5. That surgery was performed by Dr. Werts, a well-known cardiologist.
6. Jack's Toyota was made by someone in Japan.
7. This sweater was handmade by my grandmother.
8. Hundreds of thousands of faxes are sent every day by fax machines.

Delete the agents in these sentences if it can be done without significant loss of information.

EXAMPLES: The surgery was performed by the surgeon without the proper authorization.

The surgery was performed without the proper authorization.

That city was almost destroyed by a hurricane.

(Agent cannot be deleted)

1. The theory of relativity was discovered by Albert Einstein.

_____

_____

2. The man was rescued from the fire by his dog.

_____

_____

3. That car was built in Japan by the Japanese.

_____

_____

4. To my surprise, I was interviewed by the manager himself.

_____

_____

5. After Richard's car was hit by someone, it had to be repaired.

_____

_____

6. The pictures were taken by the photographer at the wedding.

_____

_____

7. For the first time in the history of the city, the position of mayor was filled by a woman.

_____

_____

8. The worker was injured by a falling brick.

_____

_____

In the following short story, decide whether a form of *be* or *get* is a more suitable auxiliary. It is possible that both may be correct in some cases.

Paul was sick last week, so he went to the health center at school. The doctor told him to **(1)** _____ undressed so that he could **(2)** _____ examined. Paul did as he **(3)** _____ told. The doctor was upset when he took Paul's temperature—it was 103°F! Paul **(4)** _____ sent to the hospital, where he **(5)** _____ asked a lot of questions. Finally, he **(6)** _____ taken to a private room where he stayed for three days. His illness **(7)** _____ diagnosed and he **(8)** _____ treated. Paul **(9)** _____ cured rapidly after his doctor prescribed the correct medicine. Because he called his teachers, he didn't **(10)** _____ dropped from his classes.

EXERCISE 10   (*Focus 5*)

Certain verbs do not have an active or a passive corresponding form; write NC (no change) for these verbs in the sentences below. If the verb in the sentence can be changed from active to passive or from passive to active, write the new sentence in the space provided.

EXAMPLES: Michael died last week of unknown causes. __NC_____

The man was killed by a stray bullet. __A stray bullet killed the man.__

A thief was arrested. __The police arrested the thief.__

1. The sheriff conducted the search for the missing child.

_____

2. The child disappeared on Thursday at approximately 1 P.M.

_____

3. A postal carrier was accused.

_____

4. The postal carrier seemed innocent.

_____

5. He had a good excuse.

_____

6. He was arrested by the sheriff anyway.

_____

7. The postal carrier stayed in jail for three weeks.

_____

8. The child was found in another state.

_____

9. The child appeared to be healthy.

_____

10. The postal carrier was released from jail.

_____

11. The real kidnapper was arrested by the sheriff.

_____

EXERCISE 11 (*Focus 6*)

Underline the passive verbs in the following sentences. For each, determine why the author chose to use a passive construction and write the letter of the reason in the space below.

    A. because the agent is unknown, unimportant, or obvious
    B. to emphasize the receiver
    C. to connect ideas in different clauses more clearly
    D. to make generic explanations, statements, and announcements

EXAMPLES: Surgery <u>was performed</u> at 10 P.M. __A__

           Heart patients <u>will be required</u> to attend health lectures. __D__

1. These two lamps were donated to the museum. _____

2. Before child labor laws were passed in this country, many children worked long hours in factories. _____

3. UFOs have been reported in many countries. _____

4. Catherine is required to work on Saturdays. _____

5. Something should be done about the economy. _____

6. The driver was awarded a $2 million settlement, but the passenger received far less. ___

7. Paul will buy the suit if it can be tailored by Monday. _____

8. That story has been made into a television movie. _____

9. The police would like to question the victim's sister, if that can be done without upsetting the family. _____

10. That project has been attempted five times in 15 years. _____

Decide whether to use active or passive forms of the verbs in parentheses in the following sentences and write each correct form in the space provided. There may be more than one correct choice.

Mark sold his old house and decided to build a new house instead of buying one that was already built. While his new house **(1)** _____ (build), Mark **(2)** _____ (live) in an apartment. This week, the cabinets **(3)** _____ (hang) in the kitchen and the bedroom walls **(4)** _____ (paint). Tomorrow, the roofing material **(5)** _____ (arrive).

Mark likes to watch all of this construction work. Right now, the outside windows **(6)** _____ (install) and some of the electrical work **(7)** _____ (test). A construction manager **(8)** _____ (supervise) all of this work. This person **(9)** _____ (pay) to manage all of the different workers—plumbers, carpenters, electricians, and so on. Mark is glad that someone else **(10)** _____ (do) all of this hard work!

EXERCISE 13   (*Focus 6*)

Decide whether to use active or passive forms of the verbs in parentheses in the following sentences and write the correct form in the space provided. There may be more than one correct choice.

Computers are machines that can only understand numerical information. They **(1)** _____ (translate) ideas into numbers. To do this, ideas **(2)** _____ (write) in computer languages such as COBOL, FORTRAN, and PASCAL. Programmers, the people who write computer programs, **(3)** _____ (must, think) logically so that their programs **(4)** _____ (will, understand) by these machines. Programs **(5)** _____ (must, write) carefully so that the computer commands or instructions **(6)** _____ (will, perform) or "executed" in the correct order.

Machines like these **(7)** _____ (can, perform) many functions. Computers **(8)** _____ (use) to trade stocks in the stock market or to send people to the moon. Some computers can understand human speech. A person's voice **(9)** _____ (interpret) by a special card in the computer. Despite all of these advances, people **(10)** _____ (will, need, still) to program new ideas into computers to use them for new and exciting projects.

In the following paragraphs, Jeff describes the time he was in a serious car accident. Underline the verbs and correct those that are not in the appropriate voice. Follow the example.

                                                    was hit
<u>Did</u> I ever <u>tell</u> you about the time my car ~~hit~~ by a truck? Well, it was something! A large truck was hit the front of my car. All of the lights and the windshield shattered. The left fender of the car crushed. I was still in the car and I was scared! My cousin was got out, but I trapped inside the car. My cousin, Alice, called 911 and told to go back to the car and stay with me.

When she got back, it had been begun to rain. The clouds burst open and the temperature was dropped. When the ambulance came, the paramedic discovered that the impact broke my wrist. It had been broken when my hand was hit the steering wheel. At that moment I promised myself never to rush to work again!

Test Preparation Exercises
Units 1–4

Choose the *one* word or phrase that best completes each sentence.

1. Recently, researchers _____ new reasons why the Ancient Mayans abandoned some of their largest cities.
   - (A) were discovered
   - (B) are discovering
   - (C) have discovered
   - (D) have been discovered

2. The Secretary General's position _____ vacant for two months when it was filled.
   - (A) is
   - (B) has been
   - (C) will be
   - (D) had been

3. Currently, scientists _____ more accurate and timely ways to predict earthquakes.
   - (A) are developing
   - (B) develop
   - (C) developed
   - (D) have developed

4. Next week, diplomas and academic honors _____ at the graduation ceremonies.
   - (A) will award
   - (B) will be award
   - (C) will be awarded
   - (D) will get award

5. The demonstrators _____ demands the chancellor is forced to consider.
   - (A) are going to make
   - (B) have been making
   - (C) had been making
   - (D) will have made

6. Last year, the university's School of Education _____ five full-time scholarships to minority students.
   - (A) awarded
   - (B) has been awarded
   - (C) has awarded
   - (D) was awarded

7. The residents of that nursing home still _____ to local stores.
   - (A) are driving
   - (B) drive
   - (C) have been driving
   - (D) had driven

8. The new budget _____ by the Minister of Finance in Parliament right now.
   - (A) is proposing
   - (B) is been proposed
   - (C) is proposed
   - (D) is being proposed

9. Thomas Edison _____ that inventions were the result of "one percent inspiration and 99 percent perspiration."
   - (A) believed
   - (B) was believing
   - (C) believes
   - (D) was believed

10. Today, many Western physicians _____ the methods and the benefits of Eastern medicine such as acupuncture.

        (A) will have investigated   (C) have investigated

        (B) are investigating   (D) have been investigated

Identify the *one* word or phrase that must be changed for the sentence to be grammatically correct.

11. The impact <u>that</u> the new tuition fees <u>would have</u> on student enrollment <u>had not</u>
             A   **B**   **C**

   <u>been studying</u> before the report <u>was released</u> to the press
                             D

12. Next year, <u>as part of</u> his major, Paul <u>will be spent</u> two semesters in Florence, Italy,
             A   **B**

   <u>studying</u> the economic systems of Europe <u>during</u> the sixteenth century.
    C   **D**

13. The Centers for Disease Control <u>have announced</u> yesterday that tuberculosis <u>was</u> on the
                            A   **B**

   <u>rise</u> in urban areas of <u>the</u> United States.
    C   **D**

14. By <u>the time</u> Catherine <u>finishes</u> her university courses, she <u>will type</u> <u>more than</u> 40 term
      A   **B**   **C**   **D**

   papers.

15. It <u>was discovered</u> <u>that</u> the payroll office at the university <u>have neglected</u> to deduct
         A   **B**   **C**

   <u>state tax</u> from the salaries of the teaching assistants.
    D

16. The patient <u>responded</u> to the antibiotics <u>quickly</u> <u>which</u> the doctor <u>had prescribed</u>.
          A   **B**   **C**   **D**

17. <u>Government</u> sanctions have been <u>imposed</u> <u>on</u> the <u>first days</u> of the war.
    A   **B**   **C**   **D**

18. The <u>winning</u> photographs <u>have</u> <u>been recently</u> selected <u>by</u> the contest judges.
     A   **B**   **C**   **D**

19. <u>While</u> the operating room <u>being prepared</u>, the doctors <u>washed</u> <u>their</u> hands.
    A   **B**   **C**   **D**

20. The kind words of sympathy <u>got</u> <u>deeply appreciated</u> by the old woman, who <u>had just lost</u>
                         A   **B**   **C**

   her husband after <u>30 years of marriage</u>.
                 D

5 One-Word and Phrasal Modals

EXERCISE 1 (*Focus 1*)

The placement of the modals in these sentences is incorrect. Underline the incorrect forms and then rewrite the sentences correctly.

EXAMPLE: Why Claudia <u>won't</u> drive in the city?

Why won't Claudia drive in the city?

1. Where Claudia is able to drive?

_____

2. Does Claudia allowed to drive on the highway? No, she doesn't allowed.

_____

3. Why she can't drive at night?

_____

4. Does Claudia able to see without her glasses?

_____

5. Had Bob better get a driver's license?

_____

6. Used Juan to drive a truck in his country?

_____

7. Does Martin supposed to have car insurance?

_____

8. Had Martin better buy special car insurance for his new sports car?

_____

9. Barbara hasn't to do housework.

_____

10. Can Martin drive a truck? Yes, he can drive.

_____

Read each sentence and then identify the way each modal is used. Select one of the choices. Then write an additional sentence of your own in the same way.

EXAMPLE: Can you help me open this door?

(making offers / ⟨making requests⟩ / making suggestions)

Can you lend me your jacket?

1. Shall I put away the groceries?
(expressing advice / making promises / making offers)

_____

2. We could try that new Thai restaurant tonight.
(making suggestions / making promises / expressing advice)

_____

3. You'd better not pay your rent late.
(expressing necessity or prohibition / denying permission / making suggestions)

_____

4. Would you like me to walk you to the bus stop?
(making promises / making offers / making requests)

_____

5. You ought to try harder to get to class on time.
(making requests / making suggestions / expressing advice)

_____

6. Would you join us for some coffee?
(making offers / giving invitations / making requests)

_____

7. You're not allowed to dive in the pool.
(expressing prohibition / making suggestions / denying permission)

_____

8. Can you come to our study group meeting?
(giving invitations / expressing advice / asking for permission)

_____

9. I'll mail that letter for you.
(making suggestions / expressing intention / giving permission)

_____

10. You don't have to hand in your paper until Friday.
    (making suggestions / expressing intention / expressing advice)

    _____

11. You'd better not smoke in class.
    (expressing prohibition / making requests / denying permission)

    _____

12. I'm going to graduate, even if it takes me five years.
    (expressing obligations / expressing intentions / making suggestions)

    _____

13. Could you please turn down your stereo?
    (asking for permission / expressing advice / making requests)

    _____

14. We mustn't forget to give our teacher a thank you card.
    (expressing advice or obligation / making suggestions / expressing intentions)

    _____

15. Can you come to my wedding next month?
    (making offers / making requests / expressing invitations)

    _____

EXERCISE 3   (Focus 3)

Identify the meaning of the modal in each sentence and write the meaning in the space next to the sentence. Choose from the following:

general possibility   logical inference
impossibility   ability
future time   habitual actions in the past
prediction

Then write an additional sentence of your own for each.

EXAMPLE: Jane just got married last month, so that tall, handsome man she is dancing
            with must be her new husband. _logical inference_____

            _She must be happy, because she's smiling._____

1. You couldn't be a teacher! You look so young.

   _____

   _____

2. I may have to go out of town next week.

_____

_____

3. My family used to visit my grandfather's house near the beach every year.

_____

_____

4. Claudia can't drive on the highway.

_____

_____

5. It ought to be a nice day tomorrow.

_____

_____

6. A good student will take notes in each class.

_____

_____

7. I'm going to word process my term paper before I show it to my teacher.

_____

_____

8. Before I had my ears pierced I would always lose my earrings.

_____

_____

9. Jack must not be worried about his final exams if he's going on a trip this weekend.

_____

_____

10. You couldn't be tired! You just slept for ten hours.

_____

_____

11. The train might be late due to the rain.

_____

_____

12. The highways can be very dangerous when they are wet.

_____

_____

13. Ben wasn't able to go to the mountains since he had injured his leg.

_____

_____

14. Betty has to be really upset. She didn't even touch her chocolate cake!

_____

_____

15. Jack is about to leave on vacation.

_____

_____

EXERCISE 4 (Focus 3)

How are the modals used in each sentence? Decide whether each expresses use (requests, permission, invitation, offers, promises, suggestions, advice, obligation, and necessity) or meaning (possibility or impossibility, future time, predictions, inferences, abilities, or past habitual actions).

EXAMPLES: Can you answer the phone for me?___**request**_____

You shouldn't eat with your mouth open. ___**advice**_____

1. You must keep that bandage dry. _____

2. You shouldn't eat so much fat. _____

3. Will the library be open on New Year's Day? _____

4. You just got a ticket? You must be upset! _____

5. Can I borrow your car? _____

6. I couldn't drive when I lived in my country. _____

7. Jackie used to run five miles every day. _____

8. Karen may go to Honduras this summer. _____

9. You really ought to type your term paper. _____

10. Your package might arrive this afternoon. _____

11. Could you shut the door? _____

12. Is the cake going to be ready in time for the party? _____

13. You can't possibly mean that! _____

14. Would you like to join us? _____

15. I'll drive you to the airport tomorrow morning. _____

EXERCISE 5 (Focus 4)

Based on the meaning of each sentence below, decide whether *must* or *should* would be a better choice in the blank. You may need to use a negative form.

1. Every citizen _____ pay taxes.

2. Parents _____ read to their children.

3. You _____ smoke in a library.

4. I saw Jane at the tennis club with a tall, handsome man. He _____ be her new husband.

5. You _____ be saying things like that about a relative of yours.

6. The President has only three more days to announce his decision. He _____ be under a lot of pressure.

EXERCISE 6 (Focus 5)

PART A

You have been invited to two different parties this weekend. The first party (on Saturday) is a formal wedding reception at a very fancy country club. At the reception you are speaking to the father of the bride. You have never met him before and you would like to show how polite you are. Add the appropriate modal as in the example.

Father of the Bride: So, you went to school with my daughter. What are your plans for the future?

You: Well, sir, first I ___will___ graduate and then I _____ look for a job.

FOB: Wouldn't you like to take a year off and travel the world first?

You: Sir, I have little choice. I _____ go to work immediately since I have many college loans to repay.

FOB: You _____ look into a job at the stock exchange. I know several people who got their start at the exchange. Which do you prefer, son, stocks or bonds?

You: I'm _____ say just yet, sir. I think I need more experience before I make a decision.

Raindrops start falling. The guests begin to move indoors.

FOB: We _____ go indoors and get out of this rain.

You: Yes, sir. I quite agree.

PART B

The next day you are at a backyard barbecue at your friend's house. It is very informal. Most people are wearing casual clothes such as jeans and shorts. Some people are even barefoot. Almost everyone at this party is between the ages of 18 and 24. Add the appropriate modal as in the example.

You: When _____*are*_____ you _____*going to*_____ put the steaks on the barbecue? Everyone is pretty hungry.

Bob: I _____ get the fire started first. It keeps going out. You _____ run to the supermarket and get me some more lighter fluid.

You: I _____ do that right now. I see Jeannie's friend over near the pool. I've been trying to meet her for weeks.

Bob: Well, it's your choice. If I _____ light the fire, then we _____ to be able to eat these steaks.

You: Gotta go!

EXERCISE 7 (Focus Five)

What modal meanings are expressed by each of the following sentences? Circle the meaning you select.

EXAMPLE: Students should be able to word process their term papers. (advisability, (ability))

1. Charles may have to explain his absence. (necessity, permission)

2. He's not going to be able to pay his house payment if he buys a new car. (future activity, ability [negative])

3. Children have to be able to play with other children. (necessity, ability)

4. Dogs shouldn't be allowed to run free in city parks. (inadvisability, necessity [negative])

5. My neighbor will have to return to his country soon. (future activity, necessity)

6. Senior citizens ought to be able to drive. (obligation, ability)

EXERCISE 8 (Focus 5)

Decide whether the following sentences are formal or informal. Write either "F" (formal) or "I" (informal) next to each sentence.

1. Jack's gotta leave right away. _____

2. Bob must meet with his instructor today. _____

3. The governor is not able to speak with you this week. _____

4. Ray's gonna be late for the party. _____

5. May I come in? _____

6. Patrick hasta work late again. _____

UNIT

6 Infinitives

EXERCISE 1 *(Focus 1)*

Underline the infinitive and gerund forms in this passage. Write "I" (for infinitive) or "G" (for gerund) under each one. The first two sentences have been done for you.

(1) People in many countries like to celebrate Carnival. I **(2)** Dancing and laughing can be heard in New Orleans, Rio de Janeiro, and in most cities in Spain. **(3)** The residents of these cities expect to spend months practicing their special routines in "samba" schools.

(Under "to celebrate": I — under "Dancing": G — under "laughing": G)

(4) In Rio de Janeiro, most of the citizens take the time to make costumes and to prepare floats for the carnival's many parades. **(5)** Each float has a theme. **(6)** The costumes are designed to match this theme and original dances are arranged to represent this idea. **(7)** It sounds like fun, but it's really hard work to organize all of these efforts. **(8)** Practicing takes up more time each day as carnival approaches. **(9)** People skip work to learn their dances and to finish their costumes. **(10)** All work is to be completed by Mardi Gras, or "Fat Tuesday," as it is known.

(11) In New Orleans, residents compete to be named "king" of a "Crewe" or float. **(12)** Competition is fierce and future kings are required to prove that they have enough money to pay for the Crewe. **(13)** Building the Crewe and designing and paying for costumes are all part of the king's job.

EXERCISE 2 (Focus 2)

Underline the infinitives in each of the following sentences. For sentences 1–4, identify the infinitive as either affirmative or negative.

1. My mother begged me not to go. _____

2. She would only allow me to stay out until 9 P.M. _____

3. I decided to live in the dorm. _____

4. I chose not to commute back and forth to campus anymore. _____

For sentences 5–8, identify the infinitive as either active or passive.

5. My new dorm room needed to be cleaned. _____

6. I went to look for my new roommate. _____

7. My boxes have to be unpacked. _____

8. I'm going to unpack one suitcase tonight. _____

For sentences 9 and 10, identify the infinitive as one of perfect or progressive aspect.

9. I would prefer to have gotten a private room. _____

10. I want to be finishing up when my roommate returns. _____

EXERCISE 3 (Focus 2)

Complete the sentences by expressing the idea in the infinitive as a verb phrase.

EXAMPLE: I hope to be given a private room in the dorm.

I hope that _____*I will be given*_____ a private room in the dorm.

1. My cousin is always content to be dropped off at a shopping mall on the weekend.

   If my cousin _____ on a weekend, she is content.

2. Anastasia claimed to have been a princess during the Tsarist period in Russia.

   Anastasia claimed that she _____ during the Tsarist period in Russia.

3. The university requires all students to sign an ethics statement before they are given access to the Internet.

   The university requires that all students _____ before they are given access to the Internet.

4. Penelope expected Morris to have done the dishes by the time she got home.

Penelope expected that Morris _____ by the time she got home.

5. The professor reminded the students not to forget to type their term papers.

The professor said, "_____."

6. We hope to be paid on the first of the month.

We hope that we _____ on the first of the month.

7. The children are happy to be left alone with their video games.

If the children _____ with their video games, they are happy.

8. I expected Paul to be waiting for me.

I expected that Paul _____ for me.

EXERCISE 4   (Focus 3)

Identify who performs the action described by the infinitive in these sentences. Write your answer in a complete sentence on the line provided.

EXAMPLE: John was asked to pick up the ice for the party.

John will get the ice.

1. Pauline promised my sister to clean up after the party.

_____

_____

2. Sally intends for Norman to lose 10 pounds by July.

_____

_____

3. The teacher encouraged us to go to the library.

_____

_____

4. The school requires all students to return library books before they can get their semester grades.

_____

_____

5. The school forced the city government to resume funding the school lunch program.

_____

_____

6. Peter dared Michael to pick the flowers in Mr. Johnson's front yard.

_____

_____

Practice using Pattern 1 verbs by completing these sentences with the infinitive form of each verb in parentheses. Sentence 1 has been done for you.

1. The thief refuses…(acknowledge his crime)

The thief refuses to acknowledge his crime.

2. He needed…(tell about the situation) (passive)

_____

3. We decided…(leave earlier)

_____

4. They appeared…(be happy)

_____

5. Would you dare…(swim during a storm)

_____

6. Raphael sometimes hesitates…(raise his hand in class)

_____

7. She should never have agreed…(send money)

_____

8. Sam refused…(be nominated) (passive)

_____

9. Do you really want…(know your future)

_____

10. Bill neglected…(pay his rent last month)

_____

EXERCISE 6 (Focus 4)

With a partner, take turns asking questions with the following verbs:

dare	refuse	hope	agree	decide
pretend	deny	wait	seem	plan

EXAMPLE: *Have you ever pretended to be someone else?*

Did you ever refuse to do something?

What are you planning to do this weekend?

EXERCISE 7 (Focus 5)

Decide whether each of the following sentences is correct ("C") or incorrect ("I"). Then correct the sentences that have been labeled with an I.

EXAMPLE: Mary convinced Sally to buy a lottery ticket. _C_

John
Paul persuaded to go with him to the baseball game. _I_
^

1. The policeman forced me to pull over. _____

2. He warned not to drive so fast. _____

3. He allowed to go without giving me a ticket. _____

4. Mark's father urged him to stay in school and graduate. _____

5. My mother hired to trim the trees and cut the bushes. _____

6. The bank encouraged the Wilsons to apply for a loan. _____

7. Mr. Tarnelli advised his daughter to set up a checking account. _____

8. Our speech teacher taught how to introduce a topic in a natural way. _____

9. The state requires to have car insurance. _____

10. My parents always encouraged me to ask questions. _____

Many Pattern 3 verbs can be followed by either an infinitive or a noun phrase plus an infinitive. Complete each of the following sentences with the verb in parentheses. Base your decision to add a noun phrase before the verb or not on the meaning of the sentence.

EXAMPLES: I like to give dinner parties, but I prefer __someone else to clean the kitchen__ (clean).

He wants me to leave, but I want __to stay__ (stay).

1. Christine needs to write her term paper, but she hopes _____ _____ (word process).

2. Beth and I are giving a party next week. I expect to pay for the food, but I expect _____ (pay for the drinks).

3. I've arranged to call the food service and the musician, but I've arranged_____ _____ (write the invitations).

4. John is good at cooking, but terrible at arranging flowers. I've asked John to do the cooking. But I've asked _____ _____ (arrange flowers).

5. Beth would like me to dress up for the party and she would like _____ _____ (buy a new dress).

Combine these sentence pairs. Replace the indicated word with an infinitive complement made from the first sentence.

EXAMPLE: Kate will spend a year in the Amazon jungle. Her parents don't want her to do **this**.

Kate's parents don't want her to spend a year in the Amazon jungle.

DUANE GILLOGLY .93

1. Kate will keep detailed notes of her research. Her professor has requested **this**.

_____

_____

2. Kate will get vaccinations before she goes. The government requires that she do **this**.

_____

_____

3. Kate has already studied the language of the Amazon tribe that she will live with. Her professor insisted on **this**.

_____

_____

4. Kate will try to learn about Amazon folk medicine. She has decided to do **this**.

_____

_____

5. Kate has already written a list of research questions. Her professor encouraged **this**.

_____

_____

6. Kate is feeling a little bit nervous before her trip. Her family expected **this.**

_____

_____

EXERCISE 10 (*Focus 7*)

Make the second noun phrase the main subject of each passive sentence.

EXAMPLE: The police forced Robert to show his driver's license.

Robert was forced to show his driver's license.

1. Kate's professor expected her to keep detailed notes.

_____

2. Kate's parents asked her to stay in the United States.

_____

3. Kate's brother encouraged her to carry a supply of vitamins.

_____

4. The university selected Martha to receive the Young Scholar's award.

_____

5. Stewart invited Martha to visit his family at the lake.

_____

6. Many people consider Stanford University to be one of the finest universities in the country.

_____

EXERCISE 11 (*Focus 8*)

When the infinitive is the subject, we usually begin such sentences with *it* and put the infinitive at the end of the sentence. Follow the example.

EXAMPLE: To listen to music is relaxing.

It's relaxing to listen to music.

1. To cook for a big family can be difficult.

_____

2. To swim on a hot day is enjoyable.

_____

3. To learn a second language when you are a child is easier.

_____

4. To have helped you is my pleasure.

_____

5. For Max to study accounting next year is a good idea.

_____

6. For Alex to postpone his trip is a wise idea.

_____

UNIT 7 Gerunds

EXERCISE 1 *(Focus 1)*

Complete each sentence by expressing the idea in the gerund (which is highlighted) as a verb phrase.

EXAMPLE: Jack's boss suspected him of **looking** for another job.

Jack's boss suspected that ____he was looking____ for another job.

1. I think that Jack resents **being spied on.**

I think Jack resents that _____.

2. Most women hate **being whistled at** by men.

When _____, they hate it.

3. I really appreciate **your having watered** my garden while I was out of town.

I really appreciate that _____

while I was out of town.

4. We didn't plan on **there being** an earthquake.

We didn't plan for the possibility that _____.

5. I enjoy not making the bed when I stay in a hotel.

_____, and I enjoy that.

EXERCISE 2   (Focus 1)

Interview a partner by asking questions on the following topics. Follow the example.

EXAMPLE: What type of books do you enjoy reading?
I enjoy reading science fiction.

1. sports you enjoy performing or watching
2. subjects you enjoy studying
3. household cleaning chores you don't mind doing
4. foods you dislike eating
5. social functions that you do not enjoy attending

EXERCISE 3   (Focus 2)

In each of the following sentences, underline the agent who performs the action described by the gerund.

EXAMPLE: We resent <u>Janice's</u> smoking in the office.

1. I don't mind having other people organize the school picnic.
2. Cynthia could never imagine Pete's leaving her.
3. Is there any way we can delay paying the bill?
4. Carol will never forgive John's having called off their wedding.
5. We didn't anticipate Phil's not being able to come.
6. Bob and I both enjoy Jack's cooking.
7. Jack has considered becoming a chef.
8. The school won't excuse Charles's being absent for a month.

EXERCISE 4   (Focus 3)

Change each verb in parentheses to the gerund form.

Americans have too much stress! Doctors recommend **(1)** _____ (relax)
and **(2)** _____ (enjoy) time with family and friends. Instead, Americans resist
(3) _____ (follow) this advice. They insist on **(4)** _____ (fill)
their weekends with projects. The average American man can't avoid **(5)** _____
(mow) the lawn, **(6)** _____ (trim) the garden, and even **(7)**_____
(paint) the house. Well, some men admit **(8)** _____ (feel) resentful that their
weekends are full of chores, but their wives are just as busy. On weekends, most women can't

help **(9)** _____ (shop) for groceries and **(10)** _____ (clean)
the house.

When do Americans relax? Well, sometimes they try **(11)** _____ (sleep)
late on the weekends or they consider **(12)** _____ (have) a party. I suggest **(13)**
_____ (get) a maid and **(14)** _____ (let) the maid do the
cleaning!

EXERCISE 5   (Focus 3)

**Underline each verb in exercise 4 that requires a gerund. Then use these verb +
gerund pairs to ask your partner questions.**

EXAMPLES: *Why do doctors recommend relaxing?*

Why can't American men avoid mowing the lawn?

Why don't they try sleeping late on the weekends?

Compare your answers with others.

EXERCISE 6   (Focus 4)

Decide whether to use a gerund or an infinitive of each verb in parentheses.

1. The nurse advised the patient _____ (to take) the medicine.

2. Diet specialists urge _____ (give up) salt and fat.

3. My friends encouraged me _____ (join) their health club.

4. The diet forbids _____ (eat) chocolate and fried foods.

5. Sally allows her sister _____ (go) running with her.

6. The health club requires you _____ (sign up) for a year.

Write two sentences for each verb using the elements in parentheses and following
the examples.

EXAMPLE: I appreciate (receive) (your letter)

I appreciated receiving your letter.

I appreciate (John) (write) (letter of recommendation)

I appreciate John's writing that letter of recommendation.

1. Katherine misses (eat) (freshly made bread)

   _____

   Katherine missed (her sister) (sing) (in the shower)

   _____

2. Benjamin understands (need) (time alone)

   _____

   Benjamin understands (his roommate) (need) (time alone)

   _____

3. I won't tolerate (receive) (torn magazines in the mail)

   _____

   Patrick won't tolerate (his mother) (get) (poor service)

   _____

4. Warren postponed (wax) (his car)

   _____

   Mr. Davis postponed (his daughter) (get married)

   _____

5. Scott denied (take) (the last piece of cake)

   _____

   The captain denied (Anthony) (take a vacation)

   _____

Discuss the differences between these sentences with a partner.

Combine each of the following sentence pairs into one sentence. Replace the indicated word with a gerund phrase made from the first sentence.

EXAMPLE: Matt will graduate in two months. Matt's mother is excited about **this.**

Matt's mother is excited about his graduating in two months.

1. Matt wants to get a good job right away. His brother doesn't understand **this.**

_____

_____

2. Matt still has two term papers to write in his last semester. He wanted to avoid **this.**

_____

_____

3. Matt eats dinner in the cafeteria. He won't miss **this.**

_____

_____

4. Matt talks about returning to Hawaii. Tom, his roommate, resents **this.**

_____

_____

5. Matt will get a new car. His parents are not looking forward to **this.**

_____

_____

6. Matt will have to pay for his own car insurance. He didn't anticipate **this.**

_____

_____

Complete each sentence by using the gerund form of the verb in parentheses.

1. _____ (jog) every day can be hard on the knees.

2. He is tired from _____ (drive) all night.

3. I would like to quit _____ (worry).

4. Cynthia's looking forward to _____ (spend) a lot of money.

5. _____ (relax) is difficult for some people.

6. Thank you for _____ (smoke [negative]).

7. _____ (stay) up all night gives you circles under your eyes.

8. Some students learn best by _____ (watch).

9. _____ (collect) sea shells is an enjoyable hobby.

10. Paul is worried about _____ (have [negative]) health benefits when he retires.

EXERCISE 10   (*Focus 7*)

Fill in each blank with the gerund or infinitive form of the verb in parentheses. There may be more than one correct answer.

When I was a child, I used **(1)** _____ (watch) TV three or four hours a day. Now my children spend hours **(2)** _____ (play) video games. Their grandmother tries **(3)** _____ (get) them to play outside. She thinks **(4)** _____ (spend) time outside is healthier for them. I agree in part, but these children are learning **(5)** _____ (use) a computer and **(6)** _____ (read) instructions. I can remember **(7)** _____ (be) bored when I was a child. I couldn't stand **(8)** _____ (watch) more reruns. But children today enjoy **(9)** _____ (select) their own videos and computer game cartridges.

My daughter prefers **(10)** _____ (play) word adventure games, where you try **(11)** _____ (imagine) the playing scene in your mind. My son, on the other hand, prefers **(12)** _____ (practice) his hand-eye coordination with sports games. They practice for so many hours that sometimes I threaten **(13)** _____ (unplug) the machine. When that happens, they usually offer **(14)** _____ (let) me play!

EXERCISE 11 (*Focus 7*)

Select the meaning implied by each of the following sentences. Circle the correct answer as in the example.

EXAMPLE: Susan remembered to lock the door.

        a. She remembered that it was important to lock the door, and then she locked it.

        b. Susan locked the door. Two years later she remembers that she locked it.

1. Patrice stopped drinking regular coffee because she suffered a heart attack.

   a. Patrice no longer drinks coffee.

   b. Patrice had a heart attack because she doesn't drink coffee anymore.

2. Maricella remembers going to her grandparents' beach house when she was a little girl.

   a. She thought about going there and then she went.

   b. She has pleasant memories of her childhood trips to the beach house.

3. Alberto forgot to bring his passport to the airport.

   a. He brought his passport to the airport, but he doesn't remember that he did.

   b. He should have brought the passport to the airport, but he didn't remember to.

4. The kindergarten teacher tried to quiet the noisy children, but they wouldn't listen to her.

   a. They continued to talk.

   b. They stopped talking, but the room was still noisy.

A small group of verbs (forget, remember, try, stop, quit, and mean) show a difference in meaning when they are used as either a gerund or an infinitive complement. In this exercise, the verb and its intended meaning are supplied for you. Write the sentence that matches the meaning.

EXAMPLE: remember, visit Paris

(I visited Paris. Now I'm remembering that visit.)

I remember visiting Paris.

1. quit, Jack, smoke

(Jack doesn't smoke anymore.)

_____

2. remember, always, lock the front door

(I never forget to lock the front door.)

_____

3. try, the classroom was cold, so the teacher, close the window

(The teacher was not able to close the window.)

_____

4. try, the window was stuck, we, turn on the heater

(The heater was our second choice.)

_____

5. forget, take, these pictures

(I took these pictures, but I can't remember exactly when.)

_____

6. stop, he, think

(He stopped what he was doing to think more clearly.)

_____

7. stop, Penny, drink coffee

(She used to drink coffee, but she doesn't anymore.)

_____

8. mean, Carl, pick up some milk, on his way home

(Carl intended to purchase some milk.)

_____

Fill in each blank with the gerund or infinitive form of the verb given. There may be more than one correct answer.

1. Sam gets nervous _____ (talk) in front of his boss.

2. My sister always tries _____ (do) too much. Unfortunately, she doesn't get it all done.

3. When Mary stopped _____ (visit) her friend, she left her keys on the kitchen table.

4. I got more and more upset _____ (listen) to the news.

5. Sarah tried _____ (put) the problem out of her mind, but it didn't work.

6. Kate stopped writing _____ (answer) the phone, but the caller had already given up.

7. I'll be happy _____ (explain) it again.

8. The child plans _____ (read) his comic books by flashlight.

9. Suddenly, Tom's elbow began _____ (hurt).

10. Hosein was at the party, but I don't remember _____ (talk) to him.

TOEFL®

Test Preparation Exercises
Units 5–7

Choose the *one* word or phrase that best completes each sentence.

1. Jennifer always has great trouble _____ her biology lab reports.
   - (A) to complete
   - (B) completing
   - (C) having completed
   - (D) to be completed

2. I know that I _____ write to my grandparents more often, but I can't seem to find the time.
   - (A) had better
   - (B) am about to
   - (C) ought to
   - (D) would

3. These days a computer is necessary for _____ term papers.
   - (A) writing
   - (B) to write
   - (C) can write
   - (D) be able to write

4. A kindly old gentleman offered _____ my bags to the taxi stand.
   - (A) his helping to carry
   - (B) helping to carry
   - (C) me to carry
   - (D) to help me carry

5. My advisor encouraged _____ a summer course to improve my writing skills.
   - (A) me to take
   - (B) for me to take
   - (C) me taking
   - (D) that I should take

6. Our senator doesn't believe that we _____ pay higher energy taxes.
   - (A) will must
   - (B) may be allowed to
   - (C) should have to
   - (D) ought to be able to

7. The design of the new space station _____ on this coming year.
   - (A) must decide
   - (B) is supposed to decide
   - (C) should to be decided
   - (D) is to be decided

8. I can't imagine _____ to such an exclusive party.
   - (A) my inviting
   - (B) being invited
   - (C) them to invite me
   - (D) to be invited

9. The admissions officer urged _____ in the application as soon as possible.
   - (A) to send
   - (B) me to send
   - (C) me sending
   - (D) my sending

10. It's so exciting for a young child _____ grown-up things like staying up late.
  (A) to do
  (B) doing
  (C) can do
  (D) that is able to do

Identify the *one* underlined word or phrase that must be changed for the sentence to be grammatically correct.

11. If you <u>are to learn</u> Japanese in a hurry, you <u>mustn't</u> <u>be allowed to</u> speak your native
        A   **B**   **C**
language <u>while</u> the training program.
      D

12. Here in the United States, <u>I'm having</u> a hard time <u>getting</u> <u>used to eat</u> dinner <u>as early as</u>
                                A   **B**   **C**   **D**
5:30 in the afternoon.

13. In <u>deciding</u> on the proper treatment, doctors <u>supposed</u> <u>to be able to</u> rely on the accuracy
      A   **B**   **C**
of the tests they <u>have ordered</u>.
              D

14. Martha knew she <u>had to</u> photocopy her income tax forms before <u>mailing</u> them, but she
                  A   **B**
was under such pressure <u>to meet</u> the deadline that she forgot <u>copying</u> them for her files.
                             C   **D**

15. <u>Taking</u> care of a baby <u>can be</u> so difficult that one parent <u>shouldn't give</u> the total
      A   **B**   **C**
responsibility for <u>doing</u> all the work.
                  D

16. The guests <u>expected</u> <u>to wear</u> formal evening clothes, but Ralph refused <u>to put on</u> his
               A   **B**   **C**
tuxedo and insisted on <u>wearing</u> jeans instead.
                        D

17. You<u>'ve got to</u> remind <u>me</u> <u>to tell</u> you the story <u>about to meet</u> my in-laws for the first time.
          A   **B** **C**   **D**

18. The security guard <u>warned to lock</u> his door, but David kept <u>forgetting</u> <u>to do</u> it, so naturally
                            A   **B**   **C**
he <u>got robbed.</u>
      D

19. On my way <u>to meet</u> my girlfriend, I stopped <u>buying</u> some flowers, when suddenly
                A   **B**
someone stopped me <u>to ask</u> for directions, and I later realized that I had forgotten <u>to pay.</u>
                      C   **D**

20. Our parents advised <u>us to take</u> advantage of <u>being</u> in the United States by <u>visiting</u>
                        A   **B**   **C**
Canada as well, so we are thinking of <u>to travel</u> to Quebec.
                                       D

UNIT 8

Statements of Degree
Intensifiers and Degree Complements

In the following passage, circle the intensifiers and underline the words they modify. The first sentence has been done for you.

(1) Peter Thatch is a *rather* accomplished architect who has been awarded several *reasonably* important contracts by companies and city governments. (2) Recently, however, he hasn't received enough work to pay his expenses. (3) His partner told him that his new designs were somewhat hard to understand. (4) At first he was extremely upset by his partner's observations. (5) Later he realized that his designs really were too complicated for most city buildings.

(6) Peter decided to rework a plan that had recently been rejected. (7) First he made the hallways slightly bigger to make it easier to deliver office equipment. (8) Next Peter added more windows. (9) This would provide quite a bit more light. (10) He redesigned the air conditioning system and the cafeteria as well. (11) Peter is quite proud of his new design and is fairly confident that it will be accepted.

Using the intensifiers in Focus 2, fill in the blanks. For some sentences there are several possible answers.

Mary is going to a dinner party at her boss's home and she is afraid that she will make a mistake. Right now she is getting dressed. She doesn't want to wear anything (1) _____ bold or stylish. She thinks that she should wear something (2) _____ boring. Scott, her date, is waiting for her and he is (3) _____ annoyed because she is taking (4) _____ much time.

Scott arrived **(5)** _____ early because he knew that this was a **(6)** _____ important occasion for Mary. Mary works **(7)** _____ hard, but she is **(8)** _____ afraid that her boss won't give her a promotion. Scott thinks that she worries **(9)** _____ much. He is becoming **(10)** _____ concerned because she hasn't finished getting dressed yet!

EXERCISE 3 (Focus 3)

Decide whether *too* or *very* is the appropriate intensifier in each of the following sentences.

1. Tom's dog barks loudly and tries to bite anyone who comes to the house. That dog is _____ aggressive.

2. Jane works full-time as a nurse's aide and she is going to nursing school. She is _____ serious about becoming a nurse.

3. The leftover food was in the refrigerator for eight days. It's _____ old to eat.

4. Bruce has been in the hospital for three months. He is getting better very slowly, but he is still _____ sick.

5. Because of their work, the Harrimans are rarely at home. They're _____ busy to plan parties or relax in the yard.

6. At $80,000, that car is a little _____ expensive for my budget.

7. The supermarket is _____ far from my house so I have to drive.

8. This lemonade is a bit _____ sweet. Next time, use less sugar.

9. William arrived at the party _____ late to have any dinner.

10. Mariko is _____ happy at her university and she plans to stay there for four years.

Complete the following sentences using an intensifier with *too*.

EXAMPLE: A cup of coffee costs $4 at that restaurant.

That's way too expensive.

1. That report was due on Monday and today is Wednesday. It's _____ late to turn it in.

2. This lemonade needs more sugar. It's _____ sour.

3. I wish John would act nicer. He's _____ rude to the workers he supervises.

4. Brian hugs everyone the first time he meets them. He's _____ friendly.

5. Arshak drives 65 m.p.h. near elementary schools! He drives _____ fast.

EXERCISE 5 (*Focus 5*)

Some ideas are very direct. They may even offend the listener because they are too direct or blunt. Sometimes we try to "soften" the idea when we present it, as in the following example.

EXAMPLE: Direct _Jerry's sister is too loud._

Softened _Jerry's sister is not shy._

Read each of the following sentences and identify them as either direct or softened. Discuss your choices with a partner.

1. Charles is too stupid to understand. _____

2. Betty is not very interested in her job. _____

3. I hate weak coffee. _____

4. The seats are too small. _____

5. That story was too long. _____

6. The soup is too salty. _____

7. The painter was not quite as neat as I would have liked. _____

8. Pauline dislikes going to museums. _____

9. The new delivery person is slow. _____

10. Janice is a terrible skier. _____

(*Focus 5*)

Soften the sentences you marked as direct in Exercise 5 with *not*.

EXAMPLE: _Charles is not bright enough to understand._

_____

_____

_____

_____

_____

_____

_____

EXERCISE 7 (*Focus 6*)

Mr. Green is Denise's boss. In this exercise you will learn about his management style. Restate the following pairs of sentences with statements of degree using *too* and *enough*.

EXAMPLES: Mr. Green is really impatient. He won't let his employees finish their sentences.

Mr. Green is too impatient to let his employees finish their sentences.

Mr. Green isn't generous. He won't give his employees a bonus for working extra hard.

Mr. Green isn't generous enough to give his employees a bonus for working hard.

1. Mr. Green was worried about delays on the new project. He asked everyone to come in on Saturday.

_____

_____

2. Mr. Green is cheap. He doesn't provide free coffee for the office workers.

_____

_____

3. Mr. Green is very busy at work. He can't take a vacation.

_____

_____

4. Mr. Green has a lot of worries. His worries keep him up at night.

_____

_____

5. Mr. Green's employees don't like him. They won't have a birthday party for him.

_____

_____

EXERCISE 8 (Focus 7)

Choose the correct implied meanings for these degree complements.

1. Peter doesn't have enough time to complete projects by next month.

   a. The projects will be completed by next month.

   b. The projects won't be completed by next month.

2. Jack has worked hard enough to get a raise.

   a. He will get the raise.

   b. He won't get the raise.

3. Janice is smart enough to avoid making a deal with him.

   a. She would never avoid making a deal with him.

   b. She avoids making a deal with him.

4. He's too old to worry about a few more wrinkles.

   a. He worries about getting wrinkles.

   b. He doesn't worry about wrinkles.

5. He's not happy enough to continue working at his present job.

   a. He's going to look for another job.

   b. He's going to stay at his present job.

Restate these pairs of sentences with statements of degree using *too* and *enough*.

EXAMPLES: Charles is very afraid. He won't ask his boss to explain the project again.

Charles is too afraid to ask his boss to explain the project again.

Alex has saved money for two years. Now he can buy a house.

Alex has saved enough money to buy a house.

1. Betty has a lot of pride. She doesn't want to ask her friend for a loan.

   _____

   _____

2. Teresa is only 15. She can't get married.

   _____

   _____

3. The office is very noisy. Mr. Addison can't concentrate on his work.

   _____

   _____

4. The cat weighs 26 pounds. He can't catch mice.

   _____

   _____

5. Pedro bought two boxes of photocopier paper. He can print his project.

   _____

   _____

6. Sam doesn't like his neighbor. He won't water her plants while she is away.

   _____

   _____

7. The little boy is 6 years old. He can go to school.

   _____

   _____

8. I am 42. I can't join the army or police force.

   _____

   _____

9. Helen always has a little extra money. She buys stocks and bonds.

_____

_____

10. Barbara has many exams. She can't help me with mine.

_____

_____

EXERCISE 10 (Focus 8)

Complete the following sentences with _so_ and _such_.

EXAMPLE: The child was ___so___ tired that he fell asleep in class.

The government provides assistance to families who don't earn enough money. Some families have **(1)** _____ little money that they can't provide enough food for their children. **(2)** _____ serious hunger is harmful to these children. They can become **(3)** _____ malnourished that their brain development is negatively affected. This problem is **(4)** _____ a serious one that the government has created an entire agency just to deal with it.

Before this agency was created, many children went to school hungry and couldn't concentrate on their lessons. **(5)** _____ a waste of human potential is a serious problem for a nation.

Warren is a high school student who works after school and also helps his mother with the gardening. He has many adult responsibilities, but he is only 16. He has **(6)** _____ a serious manner that most people think he is 18. He grew up **(7)** _____ quickly because his father died when he was 14. There were **(8)** _____ many bills to pay that Warren had to work even though he was still in high school. **(9)** _____ a situation is not unusual in the United States. Warren's mother is worried, however, since her son has **(10)** _____ little free time to study.

Restate each pair of sentences as a single sentence using *so* and *such*.

EXAMPLES: The fire spread quickly. The fire company couldn't save the house.

The fire spread so quickly that the fire company couldn't save the house.

The fire created a big mess. As a result, the street was closed for a week.

The fire created such a big mess that the street was closed for a week.

1. The Harrisons have purchased many paintings. They can't show all the paintings at one time.

   _____

   _____

2. Paul has a very easy job. He can often leave work early.

   _____

   _____

3. The earthquake caused heavy destruction. The bridge was no longer usable.

   _____

   _____

4. Carl ate six pieces of pie. He could hardly get up from his chair.

   _____

   _____

5. The government had little success with the anti-crime program. The program was canceled.

   _____

   _____

6. The carpet had become quite dirty. The carpet couldn't be cleaned.

   _____

   _____

7. The rabbits had few natural enemies in Australia. They multiplied very quickly.

   _____

   _____

8. The water hyacinth caused extensive flooding. The river had to be drained and cleared.

   _____

   _____

UNIT

9 Modifying Noun Phrases

Adjectives and Participles

EXERCISE 1   (*Focus 1*)

The highlighted modifiers in the following sentences are not in the correct order. Correct each sentence. Be sure to look at the chart in Focus 1 in your textbook.

EXAMPLE: Carlos bought **bamboo new blue two** chairs.

Carlos bought two new blue bamboo chairs.

1. We visited **a multistoried new large** office building.

   _____

   _____

2. Perry wanted to try **some French old of very that** cognac.

   _____

   _____

3. My neighbor has **little rather two spoiled** children.

   _____

   _____

4. My grandmother has **old-fashioned serving six silver** dishes.

   _____

   _____

5. My cat caught **fat really wild several** mice.

   _____

   _____

6. I returned **broken three slightly** forks to the store.

   _____

   _____

Put the adjectives in parentheses in the following sentences in the correct order.

EXAMPLE: Yesterday, Betty came home with a ___new, red silk___ (silk, red, new) dress and matching pumps.

Did she need the dress or shoes? Of course not! But don't worry, she'll return them. Last week it was the **(1)** _____ (striped, white, blue, and) vest and matching pants. She didn't keep those either. You see, Betty has to buy things because she likes to put them in her closet. Then she takes them back, still in their **(2)** _____ (store, original) wrappings.

Last week, she brought home **(3)** _____ (wool, two, expensive, very) jackets. She wanted to see if they matched her **(4)** _____ (pajama-style, wool, old) pants. Luckily one did, and she decided to keep it. The other one went back to the store along with a **(5)** _____ (white, big, round) hat and a **(6)** _____ (wool, green, bright) skirt.

Why does she do this? As the youngest of seven children, she never had new clothes. She only wore **(7)** _____ (hand-me-down, shabby, old) clothes from her older siblings. These **(8)** _____ (worn-out, ugly) garments made her look like a homeless child.

Today, Betty wears only **(9)** _____ (designer, brand-new) clothing and **(10)** _____ (leather, Italian, well-polished) shoes to match!

Write a "C" next to the correct sentences. If a sentence is incorrect, identify the problem and correct it.

EXAMPLE: It's a red, rather old Persian cat.

   ___It's a rather old, red, Persian cat.___

1. The government sent the institute a well-trained English grammar and writing instructor.

_____

_____

2. Patricia is planning her month long, next, exotic cruise.

_____

_____

3. After he left the grooming parlor, the dog had freshly clipped, gorgeous, shiny fur.

_____

_____

4. The cat caught the small brown injured mouse in the corner.

_____

_____

5. The entire family was living in a dark, one-room, tiny apartment.

_____

_____

6. The competition was held on the first floor of the government, brand-new Department of Justice building.

_____

_____

EXERCISE 4 (Focus 3)

Underline the participles (present and past) in each sentence and label them, as in the examples.

EXAMPLES: A <u>worried </u>look can signify a <u>pressing</u> problem.
past participle   _present participle_

              <u>Depressed </u>people often have <u>hidden</u> emotions.
           past participle   _past participle_

1. Pressed glass is interesting to some collectors.

2. Enduring happiness showed on her contented face.

3. Interesting secrets were revealed at the reading of the will.

4. That puzzling story led to an exciting adventure.

5. A growing child needs a balanced diet.

6. Kate was surprised by the unexpected response.

Paraphrase the sentences by choosing the correct participle for the cues given.

EXAMPLES: The jokes in the movie were rather funny.

Most of the people were ___*amused*___ (amuse) by the jokes.

The jokes were ___*amusing*___ (amuse) to most of the people.

1. The earthquake on Friday knocked down buildings and bridges. A _____ (damage) earthquake occurred on Friday. Buildings and bridges were _____ (damage) by Friday's earthquake.

2. The newspaper story revealed much personal information about the two people. The newspaper revealed an _____ (embarrass) story. The two people were _____ (embarrass) by the story.

3. The young runner received an award for finishing first. Getting the award was a _____ (satisfy) experience for the young runner. The runner was _____ (satisfy) with his award.

4. Karen didn't do well on her final exam. She was _____ (disappoint) with the exam results. The exam results were _____ (disappoint).

5. The sight of the volcano frightened the residents. The _____ (terrify) residents watched as the volcano erupted. The sight was _____ (terrify) to the residents.

Use present or past participles to complete the following definitions.

EXAMPLES: Feelings that embarrass people can be described as ___*embarrassing*___ feelings.

A room filled with many people can be described as a ___*crowded*___ room.

1. A love that endures forever can be described as an _____ love.

2. A topic that interests people can be described as an _____ topic.

3. People who show an interest can be described as _____ people.

4. A person who fascinates you can be described as a _____ person.

5. A person who annoys others can be described as an _____ person.

6. A person who worries a lot is a _____ person.

7. People who surprise you are _____ people.

8. People who show surprise on their faces can be described as _____ people.

9. News that upsets people can be described as _____ news.

10. A person who bores you is a _____ person.

EXERCISE 7   (Focus 5)

Restate the following noun phrases as nouns plus relative clauses.

EXAMPLES: a homemade cake = *a cake that is made at home*

a well-educated student = *a student who is educated to a high*

degree

1. an attention-starved child _____

2. a much-visited museum _____

3. a fast-talking salesperson _____

4. a slow-moving river _____

5. a well-known fairy tale _____

6. a fire-ravaged house _____

7. a self-made millionaire _____

8. a well-done steak _____

9. a well-timed move _____

10. fast-frozen food _____

Choose the correct participle form for each verb in parentheses from the cues given.

Communication between children and parents in the United States is often
(1) _____ (disappoint) because both parties can sometimes be unsure of the
(2) _____ (expect) outcome. The child may be **(3)** _____
(worry), **(4)** _____ (frighten), or **(5)** _____ (embarrass) about
something that the parent discovers.

The parent, on the other hand, may be **(6)** _____ (confuse) about how
to act. In one case, an **(7)** _____ (insult) word was written on a teacher's
blackboard. The boy who was **(8)** _____ (accuse) of having done this was
called to the principal's office. The boy's father was **(9)** _____ (require) to
attend this meeting as well.

The principal asked many of the **(10)** _____ (expect) questions. The
(11) _____ (frighten) child answered, but the parent wasn't
(12) _____ (interest) in his answers. He seemed **(13)** _____
(annoy) to be away from work. This attitude was **(14)** _____ (puzzle) to the
principal. He was under the **(15)** _____ (mistake) assumption that this was a
(16) _____ (concern) parent in his office. Later in the conversation, he
learned that the parent's **(17)** _____ (uninvolve) expression was his way of
hiding his own fear. This **(18)** _____ (surprise) behavior did, indeed, have an
explanation.

The **(19)** _____ (terrify) child was asked to apologize to the teacher. In
this case, counseling was **(20)** _____ (recommend) for the parent.

In a group, discuss what is "expected" behavior in each of the following situations.

Someone is arrested unjustly

A person is accused of a crime

A poor family needs help to feed its children

Use sentences starting with phrases such as

The expected behavior in this situation is…

The accused person should…

The required action is…

Concerned citizens will…

Participial phrases are reduced forms of relative clauses containing the verb *to be*. In this exercise, rephrase each highlighted participial phrase with a relative clause. Be sure to include a relative pronoun and the appropriate tense of *be*.

EXAMPLE: The woman **chatting over by the fence** is Jack's sister.

The woman who is chatting over by the fence is Jack's sister.

1. The price hike **announced last week** was the second in a year.

_____

_____

2. The reporter **planning to "break" the story** got a sudden surprise.

_____

_____

3. The criminal **arrested last week** will be tried in federal court.

_____

_____

4. The student **speaking in front of the class** is quite nervous.

_____

_____

5. The project **mentioned in the first chapter** took a year to complete.

_____

_____

6. The prize **given at the end of the week** will be the largest in the club's history.

_____

_____

Comparatives

EXERCISE 1 *(Focus 1)*

Identify the comparative structures in the following sentences. For each structure you find, identify X and Y, the features that are being compared, and decide whether X or Y is greater and whether the difference is large or small. Follow the example.

EXAMPLE: Although the rate of illiteracy in the United States is much lower than in Mexico, the United States government spends considerably more money to combat the problem.

X = <u>rate of illiteracy in the United States</u>

Y = <u>rate of illiteracy in Mexico</u>

X <u><</u> Y <u>(large difference)</u>

X = <u>United States government spending</u>

Y = <u>Mexican government spending</u>

X <u>></u> Y <u>(large difference)</u>

1. While lumber production is considerably higher in Canada than in the United States, lumber use is significantly lower in Canada.

   X = _____

   Y = _____

   X _____ Y _____

   X = _____

   Y = _____

   X _____ Y _____

2. Despite the fact that the population of the United States is nine times that of Canada, the literacy rates of the two countries show a substantially smaller difference. (United States 95%, Canada 98%).

X = _____

Y = _____

X _____ Y _____

X = _____

Y = _____

X _____ Y _____

EXERCISE 2   (*Focus 1*)

Make comparative statements using the cues given. Add an appropriate intensifier to indicate whether the difference is large or small.

EXAMPLE: land mass: South America > Australia (large)

The land mass of South America is considerably larger than that of Australia.

1. Number of castles: United States < France (high)

   _____

2. Number of castles: France > United States (high)

   _____

3. Land area: New Mexico (121,666 square miles) > Arizona (113,909) (large)

   _____

4. Land area: Arizona (113,909 square miles) < New Mexico (121,666) (large)

   _____

5. Total size: Alaska (589,757 square miles) > Rhode Island (1,214 square miles) (big)

   _____

6. Total size: Rhode Island (1,214 square miles) < Alaska (589,757 square miles) (big)

   _____

7. Achieved statehood: Alaska (Jan. 3, 1959) > Hawaii (Aug. 21, 1959) (early)

   _____

8. Achieved statehood: Hawaii (Aug. 21, 1959) < Alaska (Jan. 3, 1959) (early)

   _____

Identify the comparative structures in the following sentences. For each structure identify X and Y, the features that are being compared, and tell whether the difference is large or small. Follow the example.

EXAMPLE: At 1,306 miles (in length) the Ohio River is only slightly longer than the Columbia River (1,243 miles).

X = __Ohio River__

Y = __Columbia River__

Feature: __length of river__

X __>__ Y __(small difference)__

1. California (158,693 square miles) has much more land area than Connecticut (5,009 square miles).

   X = _____

   Y = _____

   Feature: _____

   X _____ Y _____

2. Indiana (36,097 square miles) has slightly less land area than Kentucky (39,650 square miles).

   X = _____

   Y = _____

   Feature: _____

   X _____ Y _____

3. The earth (one moon) has substantially fewer moons than Jupiter (17 moons).

   X = _____

   Y = _____

   Feature: _____

   X _____ Y _____

4. One cup of sherbet (4 grams of fat) doesn't have nearly as much fat as one cup of ice cream (14 grams of fat).

X = _____

Y = _____

Feature: _____

X _____ Y _____

EXERCISE 4   (*Focus 2*)

Make comparative statements using the cues given. Add an appropriate intensifier to indicate whether each difference is large or small.

EXAMPLE: population: United States > France (large)

The United States has many more people than France.

1. Number of immigrants: New York City > Fargo, North Dakota (very large)

_____

_____

2. Air pollution: New York City < Los Angeles (small difference)

_____

_____

3. Heavy: elephant > horse (big difference)

_____

_____

4. Expensive: plane ticket from Los Angeles to Paris > plane ticket from Los Angeles to San Francisco (large difference)

_____

_____

5. Tall: Catherine is 5'2" < Marie is 5'3" (small difference)

_____

_____

Underline the statements of similarity and difference in the following sentences. For each comparative structure you find, (a) identify the things that are being compared, and (b) decide whether the comparison describes things that are identical, similar, or different. Follow the example.

EXAMPLE: <u>His voice</u> was tired, but <u>his face</u> was happy.

(a) _his voice and his face_

(b) _different_

1. Although Jack has taken many different types of medicine, one medicine has had almost the same effect as the other.

(a) _____

(b) _____

2. Red wine and white wine have exactly the same effect on Bob.

(a) _____

(b) _____

3. Students who don't have to work have a much different educational experience than those who must work.

(a) _____

(b) _____

4. The United States and Panama use the same official currency.

(a) _____

(b) _____

5. There is a large difference between their two ideas; one is simple and the other is quite complex.

(a) _____

(b) _____

6. His voice is almost the same as his brother's.

(a) _____

(b) _____

Underline all the comparatives and statements of similarity and difference in the following sentences. For each one, answer these questions:

(a) What is being compared?

(b) Do the statements indicate that the issues being compared are identical, very similar, somewhat similar, different, or very different?

(c) What words or structures convey this information?

EXAMPLES: Scientists who study families will agree <u>that no family is exactly the same as any other</u>.

(a) _families_

(b) _different_

(c) _no family is exactly the same_

Psychologists often look at the structures of families. They compare <u>households that have somewhat the same family structures</u>.

(a) _households_

(b) _somewhat similar_

(c) _somewhat_

1. Psychologists have found that people who are from very different family structures often don't marry each other or have troubled marriages.

   (a) _____

   (b) _____

   (c) _____

2. Psychologists have also found that couples who are from the same or similar family structures understand each other better and have happier marriages.

   (a) _____

   (b) _____

   (c) _____

3. Couples with marital problems often have somewhat similar patterns of behavior.

   (a) _____

   (b) _____

   (c) _____

4. A woman who does not like her father may marry a man who has a similar problem with his mother.

    (a) _____

    (b) _____

    (c) _____

5. Couples who are from the same type of family structure will often follow the examples of their parents.

    (a) _____

    (b) _____

    (c) _____

6. People who have very different educational levels often do not have successful marriages, at least in western countries.

    (a) _____

    (b) _____

    (c) _____

7. Happy couples are usually those in which the partners have similar interests or spend their time together.

    (a) _____

    (b) _____

    (c) _____

8. Couples who fight or argue frequently often argue because they have completely different expectations of the other person's behavior.

    (a) _____

    (b) _____

    (c) _____

9. Couples who are of the same religion will have one less thing to argue about.

    (a) _____

    (b) _____

    (c) _____

10. Married people who are in the same age range will probably share many common beliefs.

    (a) _____

    (b) _____

    (c) _____

Change these informal comparisons to their more formal variations.

1. The eating habits of the French are quite different than Americans'.

_____

_____

2. Charles had much the same experience that Mitchell did.

_____

_____

3. Europeans drive differently than Americans.

_____

_____

4. Patrick's writing style is not so different from mine.

_____

_____

5. Washington state has much the same number of rainy days that Oregon does.

_____

_____

6. Health-conscious people eat differently than other people.

_____

_____

7. The society opinions about raising children in North America are quite different than in Asia.

_____

_____

8. I ate the same lunch that Jeff did.

_____

_____

TOEFL®

Test Preparation Exercises
Units 8–10

Choose the *one* word or phrase that best completes each sentence.

1. The World Trade Center in New York is _____ the Sears Tower in Chicago.
   - (A) not more tall than
   - (B) not quite the same tall as
   - (C) almost tall enough as
   - (D) nearly as tall as

2. He thinks the government hasn't been _____ about reducing the budget deficit.
   - (A) enough serious
   - (B) sort of serious
   - (C) serious really
   - (D) serious enough

3. On warm summer days we like to have a picnic under _____ tree in our yard.
   - (A) a tall old apple fragrant
   - (B) a fragrant apple tall old
   - (C) an old tall fragrant apple
   - (D) a fragrant tall old apple

4. This used to be a lively place, but everyone moved away, and now it's a _____ town.
   - (A) desert
   - (B) desert's
   - (C) deserted
   - (D) deserting

5. Venus, _____, goes around the sun in 225 earth days.
   - (A) somewhat more little than the earth
   - (B) slightly smaller than the earth
   - (C) not nearly smaller than the earth
   - (D) not much small as the earth

6. Leading economic indicators show that the rate of inflation was _____ higher than usual last month.
   - (A) very
   - (B) slightly
   - (C) too
   - (D) awful

7. The _____ girl asked her father an embarrassing question.
   - (A) precocious, cute, ten years old
   - (B) cute ten-year-old precocious
   - (C) cute, precocious ten-year-old
   - (D) ten-years-old precocious

8. Now we need to go to the _____ food section of the supermarket.
   - (A) freeze
   - (B) freezed
   - (C) freezing
   - (D) frozen

9. This airline is _____ in buying out a smaller airline to form a bigger, more competitive company.
   - (A) enough interested
   - (C) extremely interested
   - (B) too much interested
   - (D) so interested

10. I'm sorry that I missed the *Ebony Tower*, _____ shows.
   (A) some British television beautifully filmed
   (B) one of those beautifully filmed British television
   (C) the television beautifully British filmed British filmed
   (D) three British, beautifully filmed, television

Identify the *one* underlined word or phrase that must be changed for the sentence to be grammatically correct.

11. <u>Though</u> Jerry is <u>too</u> shy, he walked out on stage <u>as cool as</u> a cucumber and sang <u>like</u> he
      A   B   C   D
    had been doing it all his life.

12. The professor gave the class <u>enough time</u> and <u>too easy</u> questions, <u>yet</u> Yuriko did not do
                                   A   B   C
    <u>well enough</u> to pass the final.
      D

13. This was an <u>exciting</u>, <u>action-packed</u> war movie, but it was also <u>quite a</u> <u>thought-provoked</u> one.
               A   B   C   D

14. Choosing a <u>reasonably good</u> college is a <u>rather</u> difficult decision, <u>so</u> <u>is choosing</u> a major.
               A   B   C   D

15. It's <u>fairly</u> too hot <u>to go out</u> walking now, <u>so</u> let's go to a <u>cool, nearby movie</u> house instead.
       A   B   C   D

16. Barbara likes <u>neither reading</u> <u>heart-rending</u> romance novels nor <u>really</u> <u>shocking</u>
                      A   B   C   D
    supermarket magazines.

17. Daniel studies <u>intensely enough</u> at school <u>also</u> he is <u>quite a</u> conscientious worker at his
                   A   B   C
    <u>boring, part-time</u> job.
     D

18. We have <u>so little</u> time and <u>so many</u> things <u>to do that</u> we had better get started before it
            A   B   C
    is <u>late enough</u>.
       D

19. <u>Both</u> our <u>world-renowned company</u> president and his <u>nice, sweet-tempering</u> wife are
     A   B   C
    <u>well-loved</u> by the employees.
       D

20. Because there aren't <u>enough medical supplies</u> or <u>enough trained</u> staff, <u>so</u> doctors in
                          A   B   C
    remote areas of Africa see <u>a lot of</u> suffering that could easily be avoided.
                             D

UNIT

11 Connectors

Identify the form (coordinating conjunction, sentence connector, or subordinating conjunction) and the general meaning of each highlighted logical connector. The first sentence has been done for you as an example. Write the information between the lines.

EXAMPLE: *in order to*: form = ___subordinating conjunction___

meaning = ___cause & effect___

(1) Mark realized that he needed to meet with his advisor **in order to** get a signature on his study list. **(2) First** he tried to call his advisor's office. **(3) After** waiting on hold three times, Mark decided to walk over to the Administration Building. **(4)** There was a long line, **but** he waited. **(5) Consequently,** he stood in line for two hours. **(6)** Mark didn't want to leave without a signature. **(7) Then** he would feel as if he had wasted his time.

(8) Eventually, he met with Mr. Campanile, his advisor, **and** got his signature. **(9) As a result,** Mark was eligible to register. **(10) However,** this was not a guarantee that he would get all of the classes that he needed. **(11) While** some classes were open to all students, other classes required the signature of the instructor. **(12) In fact,** two of the classes that Mark wanted were "Signature Only" classes. **(13)** Mark found out that **besides** getting the instructor's signature, he needed to explain why he wanted to be added to each class. **(14)** He would have to make appointments with two more people. **(15) Furthermore,** these instructors might not sign his add cards. **(16) If** that happened, he would have to go back to his advisor **and** make a new study list.

(2) First : form = sentence connector   meaning = cause & effect.

(3) After : form = subordinating conjunction   meaning = sequence.

(4) but : form = coordinating conjunction. meaning = contrastive.

(5) Consequently : form = sentence connector   meaning = cause and effect.

(6) (7) Then   : form : sentence connector   meaning = cause and effect.

(8) Eventually : form : sentence connector   meaning = sequence.

and   : form : coordinating conjunction   meaning = sequence.

(9) As a result : form : Sentence connector   meaning = cause & effect.

(10) However : form : sentence connector   meaning = contrastive

(11) While : form : subordinating conjunction   meaning = contrastive

(12) In fact : form : sentence connector   meaning = additive.

(13) besides : form : subordinating conjunction   meaning = additive

(15) Furthermore : sentence connector / additive

(16) If : subordinating connector / caus & effect.

and : coordinating conjunction sequence.

Choose and underline an appropriate logical connector from the options in parentheses. There may be more than one correct choice.

(1) Both Northern and Southern California have mountains and a beautiful coastline, (and / but / furthermore) the two halves of this state have a number of differences. **(2)** Southern California, (however / on the one hand / consequently), is famous for oranges, Hollywood, and the movie and television industries. **(3)** Northern California, (therefore / however / on the other hand), is famous for its wine production, San Francisco, and its wonderful national parks.

Most residents of either half of the state will be happy to tell you why their half is better than the other. **(4)** (Nevertheless / In fact / So / In addition), they may even argue with you **(5)** (since / if / due to) you disagree with them. **(6)** (Yet / However / Moreover), most California residents travel around the state on vacation.

Recently, some people have suggested that Northern and Southern California be split into two states, **(7)** (but / on the other hand / however) where would the split occur? Which cities in the middle of the state would go into which state? **(8)** (Furthermore / Moreover / In addition), what would each new state be called?

This proposal will probably not take place. **(9)** Such a split would be complicated (and / in addition to / but also) expensive. **(10)** (Not to mention / Besides / As a result) then what would Californians have to complain about?

Circle the coordinating conjunctions in this passage and underline the elements that each connects. The first two have been done for you.

(1) Janice is <u>happy</u> and <u>nervous</u> today. **(2)** <u>Her mother is flying to Los Angeles from New York</u> and <u>will be staying with her</u> for two weeks. **(3)** Janice cleaned her apartment until it was shining and spotless. **(4)** <u>She was going to get flowers</u>, but <u>she didn't have time.</u> **(5)** On her way to the airport, <u>she thought about making reservations for dinner</u>, but <u>she wasn't sure if her mother would prefer Chinese</u> or Thai food. **(6)** She knew that her mother liked neither pepper nor curry.

(7) Once she was on the road, <u>Janice turned on the radio</u> and <u>realized that her mother</u>

was going to be late. **(8)** The weather was good in L.A., but snow near Chicago had caused a delay. **(9)** Janice had time to go shopping or to sit in a cafe and read a book.

(10) An hour later, Janice again headed toward the airport and she took her time. **(11)** She was very surprised to see her mother waiting outside for a taxi! **(12)** Her mother had heard about the Chicago snow storm and decided to take an earlier flight. **(13)** She didn't have time to call Janice, but she knew that Janice was careful and would probably call the airline for flight information.

(14) What a mix-up! **(15)** Janice could have gotten to the airport earlier but she didn't. **(16)** Her mother could have called from the plane, but she didn't. **(17)** They were both hungry and tired. **(18)** Janice offered to take her mother to either a Chinese or a Thai restaurant, but her mother just wanted to get to Janice's apartment and take a nap!

EXERCISE 4   (Focus 2)

Add the appropriate conjunction—*and*, *but*, *or*, or *nor*, to each of the following sentences.

1. Janice lives in Los Angeles, __but__ her mother doesn't.

2. Her mother will visit __and__ will stay at her place.

3. Janice was going to make reservations at either a Chinese __or__ a Thai restaurant.

4. Janice's mother likes food that is neither hot __nor__ spicy.

5. The weather was good in L.A., __but__ there was bad weather near Chicago.

6. Janice thought that she had enough time to go shopping __and__ have coffee.

7. Janice's mother had changed her flight, __but__ she didn't call Janice to tell her.

8. Janice's mother thought that Janice would call the airline __and__ she would be on time for the other flight.

9. Neither Janice __nor__ her mother had called.

10. One __or__ both of them should have called.

Combine the following pairs of sentences to make them less redundant. There is more than one way to combine some of the sentences.

EXAMPLE: Carl is blond. Anne is blond.

Both Carl and Anne are blond.

Carl is blond and Anne is too.

1. Karen likes to drink strong coffee. Margaret doesn't like to drink strong coffee.

Karem likes to drimk strong coffee, but Margaret doesn't.

2. Karen wants to go to Sea World. Margaret wants to go to Sea World.

Both Karem and Margaret want to go to Sea World.

Karem wants to go to Sea World and Margaret do too.

3. Karen likes water skiing. Karen likes diving.

Karem likes water skiing and driving.

4. Margaret enjoys water skiing. She doesn't enjoy water skiing when it is cold on the lake.

Margaret emjoys water skiing, but she doesn't emjoy —

5. Karen likes getting visits from her friends every summer. She likes getting visits from her relatives every summer.

Karem likes getting visits from her friends and relatives every summer.

6. Margaret doesn't like meeting her relatives at the airport. Karen doesn't like meeting her relatives at the airport.

Margaret doesn't like meeting her relatives at the airport, either doesn't Karem.

Combine the following sentence pairs to make them less redundant. There is more than one way to combine most of the sentences.

EXAMPLE: Kate practices yoga after work. Mary Jo practices yoga after work.

Both Kate and Mary Jo practice yoga after work.

Kate practices yoga after work, and so does Mary Jo.

1. Kate enjoys yoga. She doesn't enjoy judo.

   Kate enjoys yoga, but not judo.

2. Kate doesn't go home to change between work and her yoga class. Mary Jo doesn't go home to change between work and her yoga class.

   Both Kate and Mary Jo don't go home to change between work and her yoga class

   Kate and Mary Jo   "

3. Kate doesn't eat before her yoga class. Mary Jo eats before her yoga class.

   Kate doesn't eat before her yoga class, but Mary does.

4. Kate thinks that practicing yoga helps her to reduce stress. Mary Jo thinks that practicing yoga helps her to reduce stress.

   Kate and Mary Jo think that practicing yoga helps her to reduce stress.

5. After yoga class, Kate usually wants to eat. After yoga class, Mary Jo usually doesn't want to eat.

   After yoga class, Kate usually wants to eat, but Mary doesn't

6. The instructor wants Kate to try the advanced yoga class. The instructor wants Mary Jo to try the advanced yoga class.

   The instructor wants Kate and Mary Jo to try the advanced yoga class.

These sentences have problems with the sentence connectors. Identify the problems and correct them.

1. Although Pierre wanted to return to his native country, ~~but~~ he didn't want to leave his job here.

2. He had made a lot of money in the United States. He was able to send money to his family thus. *, so he*

3. Pierre was becoming more and more nervous about making a decision, as a result, he started smoking again. *. As a result,*

4. He started to drink heavily in addition. *In addition, ___*

5. He ~~eventually~~ went to the doctor. He ignored the doctor's advice, however.

The following sentences have problems related to the subordinating conjunctions. Identify the problems and correct them.

1. Besides I paid for the plane tickets, I also paid for the hotel. *paying*

2. Even though I offered to pay, Mary could have paid for part of the trip.

3. In spite of she didn't pay, I still talk to her. *the fact that*

4. Due to ~~she is~~ cheap, she has lost other friends. *being*

5. Since she is in all of my classes, I won't say anything to her.

UNIT

12 Relative Clauses

EXERCISE 1 (*Focus 1*)

Underline each relative clause and circle the word it modifies. Sentence 2 has been done for you as an example.

(1) Michelle has finally realized one of her lifelong dreams. (2) She has always wanted to attend the ⟨cooking school⟩ that her mentor, Chef Troisgros, attended. (3) The school, which is in Paris, accepts only 80 students every year. (4) The students who are accepted generally have at least three years of cooking experience. (5) Michelle has five years of paid cooking experience.

(6) The project that attracted the attention of Chef Troisgros, however, was a cake that Michelle made for a wedding. (7) Chef Troisgros had never tasted a cake that was as light and creamy as the one that Michelle made. (8) He gave Michelle his card and invited her to cook pastries at his restaurant beginning the next month. (9) It was this invitation that began her career baking for a big restaurant. (10) Right now she is waiting for the plane that will fly her to Paris. (11) There she will begin the three-month course that Chef Troisgros recommended.

EXERCISE 2 (*Focus 2*)

In the following sentences, circle the head noun of each relative pronoun (*that, who, whom,* or *which*). Next, draw an arrow from the noun (which you have already circled) to the place where the replaced noun has been moved. Follow the examples.

EXAMPLES: I ate ⟨a pastry⟩ that my partner had baked. ↓

I met ⟨the chef⟩ whom my chef had studied with. ↙

1. Michelle is attending the cooking course which she had dreamed about.

2. The man whom she is cooking with is an experienced cook.

3. Michelle wants to learn baking techniques that she can use back in the United States.

4. She met the man who is co-owner of the cooking school.

5. The school, which has received three blue ribbons, has been open since 1926.

6. Michelle was only recently introduced to the family whom she is now living with.

7. She bought the cookbook that was written by her teacher.

8. Every day the students eat the food that they have prepared.

EXERCISE 3 *(Focus 2)*

Combine these pairs of sentences using a relative clause with *that, who, whom,* or *which*.

EXAMPLE: Michelle started the pastry class. The cooking school recommended the class.

Michelle started the pastry class that the cooking school recommended.

1. Patrick took a course. The course is no longer offered at our school.

_____

_____

2. Kate bought a dress. The dress was on sale.

_____

_____

3. Lawrence introduced a new friend to me. He had been jogging with this friend for two months.

_____

_____

4. Michelle has a friend. Her friend owns a restaurant just outside of Paris.

_____

_____

5. I want to visit the beach. The beach was featured on a TV show.

_____

_____

6. The dog was in my backyard. The dog belongs to my neighbors down the street.

_____

_____

EXERCISE 4   (Focus 3)

Some of the following sentences are incorrect. Identify the mistakes and correct them. Also identify the sentences that are correct, and write a "C" next to them.

1. This is the person which David gave flowers.

   _____

   _____

2. My brother, that runs for two miles each morning, is in good physical shape.

   _____

   _____

3. The woman with whom he spoke had a heavy French accent.

   _____

   _____

4. The book that I read it was interesting.

   _____

   _____

5. The army troop that I mentioned earlier was ready to march after only two weeks of training.

   _____

   _____

6. The friend to whom I sent the gift was so pleased that she called me last night.

   _____

   _____

EXERCISE 5   (Focus 4)

In these sentences, delete the relative pronouns, where possible, and make the other necessary changes. (You cannot delete all the relative pronouns.)

EXAMPLES: The kind of food ~~that~~ Michelle likes to make is simple and low in fat.

I like people who like to laugh and ~~who~~ tell jokes.

1. Michelle tried to practice her baking with the student who sits near the window.

2. She examined the menus that the chef had planned.

3. She wants to return home with a diploma that was signed by Chef Lyon.

4. The student whom she had dinner with last night is from Italy.

5. She is not sure which recipe to make next.

6. Michelle prefers to make friends with people who are studying at her school.

7. Chef Lyon tasted each cake that was baked by his students.

8. The prize which is awarded to the best student is a white chef's hat.

9. Have you seen the cake that made Chef Lyon so happy?

10. Students who are near the bottom of the class may need to repeat the class in order to get a diploma.

EXERCISE 6   (Focus 5)

Combine the following pairs of sentences using *whose*.

EXAMPLE: The Sarnos own a house. The exterior of the house is frequently seen in movies.

The Sarnos own a house whose exterior is frequently seen in movies.

1. I own a cat. The cat has long fur.

_____

_____

2. Jackie bought a car from a salesman. She met his sister in the gym.

_____

_____

3. Mark often gets phone calls for a doctor. The doctor's phone number is similar to his.

_____

_____

4. I spoke to the neighbor. My son had broken his window.

_____

_____

5. The professor spoke to the student. The student's grade was lower than expected.

_____

_____

6. People may vote alike. Their thinking styles are similar.

_____

_____

EXERCISE 7   (Focus 5)

Complete the puzzle by writing the answers in the blanks. The first one has been done for you.

1. A noun form that looks like a verb.
2. A feminine pronoun.
3. A most "reflexive" word.
4. A tense that describes an action that is clearly over.
5. The opposite of "pre."
6. Clearly the opposite of passive.
7. Not ever.
8. When you pick something, you _____ it.
9. A short "stop"; not as final as a period.
10. When you get rid of a noun, you _____ it.
11. The word "_____" means silly.
12. The sign on the door says either "push" or _____ .
13. A possessive relative.
14. You circled this type of noun in Exercise 2.

```
1.    g e R u n d
2.        _ E _
3.      _ _ L _
4.        _ A _ _ _
5.    _ _ _ T
6.    _ _ _ I _ _
7.      _ _ V _ _
8.        _ E _ _ _ _

9.            C _ _ _ _
10.     _ _ L _ _ _
11.       _ A _ _ _
12.       _ U _ _
13.   _ _ _ S _
14.       _ E _ _
```

Test Preparation Exercises
Units 11–12

Choose the *one* word or phrase that best completes each sentence.

1. _____ he had been shot twice, Garrick continued to lunge at the enemy.
   - (A) However
   - (B) In spite of
   - (C) Although
   - (D) Even if

2. I finally met the neighbor _____ called the police when I had a party last month.
   - (A) whose
   - (B) who
   - (C) which
   - (D) whom

3. Veronica finished college in only three years _____ excellent advanced placement test scores and an accelerated program of courses.
   - (A) in addition
   - (B) in addition to
   - (C) as a result
   - (D) as a result of

4. Carolyn was a senior in college _____ she lost her scholarship.
   - (A) where
   - (B) of which
   - (C) when
   - (D) who

5. The company set up a free long-distance telephone number _____ customers could call with any questions they might have about its products.
   - (A) so that
   - (B) for
   - (C) therefore
   - (D) in order

6. Jake got off the freeway _____ three lanes merge into one.
   - (A) when
   - (B) that
   - (C) which
   - (D) where

7. The flag of Greece has a blue and white cross in the top left corner. _____, it has nine blue and white horizontal stripes.
   - (A) Besides
   - (B) Actually
   - (C) In fact
   - (D) In addition

8. George Orwell, _____ was Eric Arthur Blair, wrote many politically oriented novels and essays.
   - (A) that his real name
   - (B) the real name of whom
   - (C) his real name
   - (D) whose real name

9. Margaret works very hard. _____, her boss won't give her a raise.

    (A) In spite   (C) Nevertheless

    (B) Even   (D) Consequently

10. They dislike films _____ lots of action and no intellectual substance.

    (A) that have   (C) with which

    (B) that they have   (D) have

Identify the *one* underlined word or phrase that must be changed for the sentence to be grammatically correct.

11. Despite Spain ruled the Philippines considerably longer than the United States did,
    A   **B**   **C**
English is far more commonly spoken there than Spanish.
          D

12. In addition to miss her kids, Maria has realized how lonely it is to travel for business 300
    A   **B**   **C**   **D**
days of the year.

13. The Caspian Sea, in spite of its name, is a very big lake — much larger than any of the
                    A   **B**
Great Lakes; in fact, it is such large that it's bigger than the five Great Lakes combined.
          C   **D**

14. During the French Revolution, if you were sentenced to death, you were executed by
                          A   **B**
guillotine, a device was named after J. I. Guillotine, a French physician who advocated its
                 C   **D**
use.

15. Although Sandra was admitted to the hospital, but she didn't want to be there.
    A   **B**   **C**   **D**

16. Terry and Tracy look very much alike; as a result, people think they have much the same
                     A   **B**   **C**
personality when they actually think and act quite differently.
                                       D

17. In your country, what is the age when you must be to get a driver's license, providing, of
                              A   **B**   **C**
course, you pass the driving tests?
           D

18. If you have studied medieval history or philosophy, you know that Maimonides
    A   **B**
(1135–1204) was a Spanish-born Jewish philosopher and rabbi he studied Aristotle and
                                                   C
Judaic thought in order to try and synthesize them.
                 D

19. American painter Andrew Wyeth, <u>who</u> painted the famous *Christina's World*, often used

                     A

    tempera, <u>whose</u> painting technique <u>in which</u> egg yolk and water are used as an emulsion

          B   **C**

    <u>to bind</u> the colors.

    D

20. <u>Moreover</u> I have <u>gotten used to</u> the weather in this country, I prefer <u>to live</u> in <u>a more arid</u>

    A   **B**   **C**   **D**

    environment.

UNIT

13 Using Present Time

EXERCISE 1 (*Focus 1*)

Choose the correct verb tense (simple present or present progressive) to indicate whether the verbs in these sentences refer to ongoing events or to habits, skills, and recurring situations. More than one answer may be correct. Discuss your answers with a partner.

1. Pablo _____ (play) soccer on the weekends.
2. Catherine _____ (speak) on the phone right now. Please lower your voice.
3. The cat _____ (sleep) near the fireplace.
4. Karen _____ (have) trouble opening the package. Go help her.
5. Tuition _____ (go) up every year.
6. Bob _____ (do) magic tricks. Watch!
7. People _____ (wait) to board the plane to Chicago.
8. Jack _____ (get) sick at the sight of blood.
9. Your boss _____ (speak) well of you.
10. The popcorn _____ (pop) in the microwave oven.

EXERCISE 2 (*Focus 2*)

Decide whether each sentence is about a permanent or a temporary situation. Choose either the simple present or the present progressive tense to indicate the difference in meaning. Discuss the difference with a partner.

1. That stock _____ (do) well. The price went up by 50 percent yesterday.

2. I _____ (live) in the dormitory this semester.

3. Ketchup _____ (make) French fries taste better.

4. The cable television _____ (work) again. The repair person was here today.

5. Whether you _____ (want) to or not, you (have) to pay taxes.

6. No matter how hard he _____ (try), the doorman still _____ (forget) my name.

7. Mr. Gonzalez _____ (feel) happy all the time.

8. Charles _____ (feel) better since his recovery.

9. Carla _____ (search) for a summer job.

10. Bats _____ (live) in caves.

EXERCISE 3   (Focus 2)

Ask your partner a *wh*-question based on the cues given. He or she will write down your question. Then your partner will answer the question and you will write down your partner's answer.

DUANE GILLOGLY

EXAMPLES: what/crocodile/taste like

Question: ___What does crocodile taste like?___

Answer: ___It tastes like chicken.___

who/that car/belong to

Question: ___Who does that car belong to?___

Answer: ___That car belongs to Mr. Parker.___

1. which type/visa/require

   Question: _____

   Answer: _____

2. what/not like/winter

   Question: _____

   Answer: _____

3. who/resemble most/family

   Question: _____

   Answer: _____

4. what/your wallet/contain

Question: _____

Answer: _____

5. how many/shoes/own

Question: _____

Answer: _____

6. what/taking the TOEFL/require

Question: _____

Answer: _____

7. what kind of food/prefer

Question: _____

Answer: _____

8. who/that child/belong to

Question: _____

Answer: _____

9. how much/that house/cost

Question: _____

Answer: _____

10. when/realize/a problem

Question: _____

Answer: _____

EXERCISE 4 *(Focus 3)*

Decide whether the verbs in parentheses express an action meaning or a stative meaning and indicate your choice by using either the simple present or the present progressive form. In some cases, both answers are correct; discuss them with your partner.

1. The university that I want to attend now _____ (require) the TOEFL.
2. This coffee is old. It _____ (taste) like acid.
3. The chef _____ (taste) the salad dressing to see if it's fresh enough to use.
4. He _____ (mind) his own business.
5. Mary _____ (have) a baby.

6. If you ask someone how much he or she weighs, you _____ (be) really impolite.

7. I _____ (depend) on you to tell me the truth.

8. The nurse _____ (weigh) the baby in the clinic.

9. Mr. Simpson _____ (weigh) way too much for his condition.

10. He _____ (consider) taking classes in Europe next year.

11. The children _____ (be) good.

12. Good relationships between people _____ (require) trust.

EXERCISE 5   (Focus 4)

Change this story as if you were describing your own experience, using the present time frame to make it less formal. The first sentence is done for you. When you are finished, read it out loud to a partner.

So this guy ~~pushed~~ pushes me and ~~didn't~~ doesn't say he ~~was~~ is sorry. I pushed him back and he fell down on the sidewalk. When he got up, he saw that his pants were torn. He was really mad! He went to get a policeman to arrest me. He crossed the street and a cop gave him a ticket. The light was yellow and this guy crossed anyway. Well, he told his story to the cop, but the cop didn't believe him. The guy deserved it!

UNIT

14

Present Perfect
Describing Past Events in Relation to the Present

<hr>

EXERCISE 1 (*Focus 1*)

<hr>

Underline all the verbs in the following passage. Mark verb phrases that refer to general truths or recurrent actions in the present time frame "*a.*" Mark verb phrases that refer to past events that have a relation to the present "*b.*" Mark verb phrases that simply refer to completed past events "*c.*" The first paragraph has been done for you.

(1) One of the reasons that Karen <u>became</u> an ESL teacher <u>is</u> that she <u>likes</u> working with people from other countries. (2) She <u>finds</u> it very rewarding to work with her memorable experiences.

(3) Her first experience in assisting a nonnative speaker was with her grandmother. (4) Her grandmother was born in Italy and never learned much English. (5) Karen translated for her grandmother when they went shopping together. (6) In fact, she has done this for a number of her relatives.

(7) In her travels, Karen has translated for many of her fellow travelers. (8) Whenever she has helped someone, they have usually been grateful and have thanked her.

(9) As a result of her travels, Karen has experienced much the same culture shock as her students. (10) This has taught her some important lessons, especially about the first week of school.

EXERCISE 2 (Focus 2)

Decide whether you should use the past tense or the present perfect tense for each verb in parentheses. More than one answer may be correct.

Mary Morris **(1)** _____ (apply) for her passport last month. She **(2)** _____ (work) as a receptionist at Ardmore's Travel Agency for ten years. All this time, she **(3)** _____ (look) at pictures of exotic places on the wall and she finally **(4)** _____ (decide) to take an overseas trip herself.

After she **(5)** _____ (plan) her trip, she **(6)** _____ (make) her plane flights and **(7)** _____ (reserve) hotel rooms. Mary **(8)** _____ (have to [negative]) pay for her plane tickets because she **(9)** _____ (work) at Ardmore's so long.

She **(10)** _____ (want) to take this trip for a long time, but each year her vacation **(11)** _____ (cancel) because someone else **(12)** _____ (be) on vacation or someone **(13)** _____ (quit).

Mary **(14)** _____ (hear) about many exciting vacations over the years. Her boss, Ben, **(15)** _____ (be) to Japan, Kenya, Alaska, France, and Moscow! Meanwhile, Mary **(16)** _____ (see, just) his travel photos! The last time Ben **(17)** _____ (bring in) his travel pictures, Mary **(18)** _____ (resolve) to take a trip of her own.

EXERCISE 3 (Focus 3)

Do these sentences refer to situations that include the present moment or situations that were fully completed in the past? Indicate which by choosing the present perfect or the past tense for each verb. More than one answer may be correct, so be prepared to explain why you have chosen each answer.

Mark is very confused. He **(1)** _____ (discover, just) that the college **(2)** _____ (cancel) his accounting class. He's **(3)** _____ (made, already) his class schedule. Mark **(4)** _____ (return, just) from summer vacation when he **(5)** _____ (open) his mail, he **(6)** _____ (read) the bad news. His roommate **(7)** _____ (tell) him not to worry. He said, "The college **(8)** _____ (do) this before, you know. Last year, when enough students **(9)** _____ (complain), the college **(10)** _____ (put) the class back in the schedule. My guess is that the situation **(11)** _____ (change [negative]) much since then."

Choose the sentence (a or b) that reflects the most logical continuation of ideas expressed in the first sentence. Bear in mind that both sentences are grammatically correct.

1. I've *told* you that I'm allergic to pepper.

   a. So why did you put chili pepper in the soup?

   b. I'm not fond of carrots either.

2. Jack has been staying up very late.

   a. He turns on a lot of lights.

   b. He has dark circles under his eyes.

3. Maria has just given birth to twins.

   a. She likes children.

   b. She is very tired, but happy.

4. Many psychologists have observed that children of nervous mothers cry more frequently.

   a. This is an important fact for a pediatrician to know.

   b. So choose your mother carefully.

5. Mr. Wilson left the hospital two weeks ago.

   a. He has been resting at home since then.

   b. He didn't like the hospital food.

6. The Department of Health has released the list of the restaurants that were closed this month.

   a. It's a long list.

   b. Don't eat at these restaurants.

(Focus 5)

Choose either the present perfect or present perfect progressive to talk about the following events. More than one answer may be correct.

1. Catherine _____ (paint) her room. She still has to paint the windows and above the door.

2. The city _____ (charge) apartment owners for that service.

3. Bob _____ (know) about the problem for quite some time.

4. Bob _____ (ask) me about that problem for several days.

5. The water in the bathroom _____ (run) all night.

6. Mr. Lane _____ (want) to tell you about his results since he received the news. He _____ (call) three times.

7. The manager _____ (try) to solve that problem for the last six hours.

8. The delay in receiving that product _____ (result) in unhappy customers and lost sales.

9. The water in that pool _____ (smell) bad for about two days.

10. I _____ (dream) of having a free weekend for some time now.

(Focus 5)

Decide whether to use the simple present, present progressive, present perfect progressive, or past tense for each verb in this passage. More than one answer may be correct.

Janice **(1)** _____ (consider) changing careers. Right now, she **(2)** _____ (think) about going to law school. She **(3)** _____ (be) a legal secretary for five years now and she **(4)** _____ (enjoy) working with lawyers. She actually **(5)** _____ (like) the fast pace of work. In her old job, she **(6)** _____ (be) bored. Janice **(7)** _____ (have [negative]) a dull day since she **(8)** _____ (start) working for this office. But she **(9)** _____ (begin) to think about her future.

UNIT 15

Future Time

Using Present Tenses, Using *Will*
Versus *Going To* Versus *Shall*,
Adverbial Clauses in Future

EXERCISE 1 (*Focus 1*)

Underline the verbs in the following sentences. Write "P" for present or "F" for future under each verb. The first one has been done for you.

1. Each year, the swallows <u>return</u> to Capistrano.
                  P

2. Carl is bringing his guitar to the party on Saturday.

3. I might take a dance class next quarter.

4. She's having a baby sometime next month.

5. He tells the same story each time.

6. When I get my degree, I'll get a good job.

7. Look at the sky! It could rain any minute.

8. Pat's staying here.

9. My next class starts in ten minutes.

10. Everyone else is wearing a suit on Saturday. Why can't he?

EXERCISE 2 (*Focus 2*)

Choose the best tense (present/present progressive or a modal of prediction) for each verb in the following sentences. It is possible that both forms are grammatically correct, so be prepared to explain your choices.

    EXAMPLE: The bus ____*leaves*____ (leave) at 2:00. Make sure you are on it.

1. Susan _____ (graduate) if she passes her finals.

2. Next year _____ (be) my tenth anniversary.

3. We _____ (go) to Paris if I can buy inexpensive airline tickets.

4. It _____ (rain) tomorrow. Check the weather report before you leave.

102   Unit 15

5. Kenji _____ (leave) for Japan next week.

6. Paulette _____ (win) the race. She's strong.

7. We're _____ (go) to the Grand Canyon this summer.

8. April first _____ (be) April Fool's Day.

EXERCISE 3 (*Focus 3*)

Decide which form, *will* or *be going to*, should be used in the following sentences. In some cases, both answers may be correct.

1. Different people need different types of exercise. Jogging **(A)** _____ (hurt) someone with a neck or back problem. Someone with this type of injury **(B)** _____ (do) better with walking. My neighbor **(C)** _____ (to begin) an exercise program next week, but with his bad back I know it **(D)** _____ (include [negative]) jogging.

2. When **(A)** _____ you _____ (fix) that old car of yours? It **(B)** _____ (run [negative]) unless you fix it. I **(C)** _____ (be seen [negative]) in such an awful car. In fact, maybe I **(D)** _____ (buy) my own car.

3. Janice doesn't know what she **(A)** _____ (do) next month. Her temporary job **(B)** _____ (end). She **(C)** _____ (have [negative]) another project assigned to her right away. What **(D)** _____ her landlord _____ (say) when the rent is late?

EXERCISE 4 (*Focus 4*)

Decide whether *will*, *be going to*, or *shall* is a better form to use in the following sentences.

1. I _____ drive you to school if you need a ride.

2. Kathy _____ accept that salary. She's no fool.

3. _____ I give you a hint?

4. When _____ you take your vacation?

5. _____ we go?

Answer the questions below and give a brief explanation for your thinking. Use the modal in parentheses to answer each question.

    EXAMPLE: What will you be doing next summer? (may)

    I may be working for my cousin because his business is doing well.

1. Will the population of your home city increase? (will)

   _____

   _____

2. Will more people begin to use computers? (should)

   _____

   _____

3. Will the government provide low-cost day care for children? (may)

   _____

   _____

4. What will happen if you don't get all of your classes next semester? (will)

   _____

   _____

5. Will you always have the same career? (may [negative])

   _____

   _____

6. Will there be a cure for cancer? (could)

   _____

   _____

7. Will your sister like her present? (should)

   _____

   _____

8. Will the government get rid of taxes? (won't)

   _____

   _____

In each of these pairs join the second sentence to the first using the suggested linking word. Be sure to change nouns to pronouns when necessary. Remember to look at the tense of the adverbial clause.

EXAMPLE: I'll buy that desk. It will go on sale. (when)

I'll buy that desk when it goes on sale.

1. Paul and Kathy are going to have a good time. They will be on vacation in Montreal. (while)

2. I'm going to go camping for three days. I will have finished all of my final exams. (once)

3. Carl and Alicia are leaving for their new jobs. They'll sell their house. (as soon as)

4. Even my boss is going to take time off. He will have finished printing and checking the month-end report. (when)

5. The cruise will be over. We will realize how much money we spent. (before)

6. It will be almost the next semester. Carol will finally get her paper typed. (by the time)

7. He's going to go skiing. He will get a book of discount ski lift tickets. (when)

8. Janet will read her book. The baby will be napping. (while)

Complete the following paragraph. Decide whether to use the present or future form for each verb in parentheses. Consider carefully the meaning of each sentence.

Mary **(1)** _____ (travel) around Asia before she **(2)** _____ (return) home. By the time she **(3)** _____ (get) to Japan, she **(4)** _____ (have) flown 6,000 miles. As soon as she **(5)** _____ (arrive) in Japan, she **(6)** _____ call) her mother. Then she **(7)** _____ (go) to Hong Kong to pick up some pearls. When she **(8)** _____ (leave) Hong Kong, her last flight **(9)** _____ (stop) briefly in Hawaii. While the plane refuels in Hawaii, Mary **(10)** _____ (sleep). The final segment of her trip **(11)** _____ (end) in Los Angeles. When the plane **(12)** _____ (touch) down in the Los Angeles airport, Mary **(13)** _____ (be, finally) home.

TOEFL®

Test Preparation Exercises
Units 13–15

Choose the *one* word or phrase that best completes each sentence.

1. When I _____ home, I will take a long hot bath.
   - (A) will get
   - (B) get
   - (C) will be
   - (D) will have arrived

2. Marianne _____ much better when she is giving than when she is receiving presents or praise.
   - (A) feel
   - (B) use to feel
   - (C) feels
   - (D) is feeling

3. I _____ reading the play yet, and I don't want to see the performance until I'm done.
   - (A) haven't finished
   - (B) am not finishing
   - (C) won't finish
   - (D) don't finish

4. The company has been hit hard by the economic recession, so to cut costs they _____ 200 workers.
   - (A) lay off
   - (B) would lay off
   - (C) had laid off
   - (D) are laying off

5. Even though it wasn't scheduled for this program, the orchestra should be able to play Mahler's First, since they _____ it numerous times in the past couple of seasons.
   - (A) played
   - (B) have played
   - (C) are playing
   - (D) play

6. Now that she is out of a job, Aisha _____ going back to school, but she hasn't decided yet.
   - (A) considers
   - (B) considered
   - (C) has been considering
   - (D) is going to consider

7. The snow _____ soon after midnight, so the roads should be in pretty good shape for the morning rush hour.
   - (A) stops
   - (B) stopping
   - (C) has stopped
   - (D) will stop

8. Marcel Proust once said, "The only paradises _____ lost paradises."
   - (A) are
   - (B) are being
   - (C) will be
   - (D) have

9. _____ have dinner with me sometime?
   (A) Will you like to   (C) Shall you
   (B) Will you   (D) Do you

10. After four years of college, Jeremy _____ $40,000 in college loans.
    (A) is owing   (C) owes
    (B) has owed   (D) will be owing

Identify the *one* underlined word or phrase that must be changed for the sentence to be grammatically correct.

11. The Burkes <u>are going</u> to stay in a hotel <u>while</u> their house <u>will be</u> <u>renovated</u>.
               A   **B**   **C**   **D**

12. When someone <u>died</u>, it <u>is</u> customary in the United States to send flowers <u>to express</u>
                A   **B**   **C**
    sympathy, especially if it <u>is</u> not possible to attend the wake or the funeral.
                               D

13. If he <u>is</u> successful, Renato <u>will have raised</u> $200,000 <u>by when</u> the fundraising drive <u>ends</u>.
          A   **B**   **C**   **D**

14. Listen! That <u>is</u> our song they <u>play</u> on the radio, <u>so</u> <u>will you get</u> out of the car and dance
                  A   **B**   **C**   **D**
    with me?

15. Vivian's mother <u>seems</u> less and less able to take care of herself; Vivian <u>is knowing</u> that
                 A   **B**
    she <u>will</u> have to put her mother in a nursing home soon whether she <u>likes</u> it or not.
         C   **D**

16. Someday I <u>cross</u> the Sahara Desert as I <u>dreamed</u> I would when I <u>lived</u> in West Africa, but
               A   **B**   **C**
    that may have to wait until I <u>have saved</u> enough money.
                             D

17. Because the bedroom <u>measures</u> only 10 by 10 feet, Mark <u>is measuring</u> all the other
                     A   **B**
    furniture <u>in order to</u> determine whether or not a double bed <u>is fitting</u> in there.
           C   **D**

18. Ever since he <u>piloted</u> a medical evacuation helicopter in the Vietnam War, Buzzy <u>isn't</u>
               A   **B**
    able to drive or fly any kind of vehicle, nor <u>can he stand</u> the sound that helicopters <u>make</u>.
                                     C   **D**

19. Mona <u>has been trying</u> to rewrite her composition , but she <u>has not been able to</u> because
             A   **B**
    she <u>has been feeling</u> that the teacher did not give her enough feedback about what <u>was</u>
          C   **D**
    wrong with the first draft.

20. Lucas <u>is having</u> a meeting with Hiro next week at which they <u>are going to</u> discuss a new
        A   **B**

movie project about a small-town boy and girl who grow up together as friends but

<u>do not realize</u> that they <u>are loving</u> each other.
     C   **D**

UNIT
16 Modals of Prediction and Inference

Make sentences from the given cues, using modals.

EXAMPLE: Meaning: It will possibly happen.

Carl's cousin Ted/wants to go out to dinner

Carl's cousin Ted may want to go out to dinner.

1. Meaning: It is likely to happen.
   Pat/decide where to go on vacation

   _____

2. Meaning: It certainly won't happen.
   Pat/want to take his mother-in-law along

   _____

3. Meaning: It will possibly not happen.
   He/even tell her about the trip

   _____

4. Meaning: It will certainly happen.
   His wife/tell her mother

   _____

5. Meaning: It will possibly happen.
   They/ask the mother-in-law to watch their house

   _____

6. Meaning: It will quite possibly happen.
   She/look in all of their closets

   _____

7. Meaning: It is somewhat possible that this might/will happen.
   It/rain heavily tonight

   _____

8. Meaning: It will certainly not happen.
   That student/be able to finish on time

   _____

9. Meaning: It is not likely that this will happen.
He/expect a tax refund

_____

10. Meaning: It will certainly happen.
That sick child/cry all night

_____

EXERCISE 2   (Focus 2)

Fill in each blank with an appropriate modal of inference. There may be more than one correct answer, and some may have negatives.

1. I thought I heard a knock on the door. It **(A)** _____ be my son. He usually comes home around now. Or it **(B)** _____ be my mother-in-law. It **(C)** _____ even be my husband. No, he never knocks.

2. Where have I put my keys? They **(A)** _____ be in this room. They **(B)** _____ just walk away. They **(C)** _____ be near the sink, since I washed my hands when I came in from the garden. Or they **(D)** _____ be in the pockets of my gardening pants.

3. Andrew looks upset. He was sick for three weeks and now he **(A)** _____ fail his chemistry class. He **(B)** _____ have talked to the professor before. Now he **(C)** _____ make up his chemistry lab assignments because it's too late. Now he **(D)** _____ go to the Dean of Students and explain his problem.

EXERCISE 3   (Focus 2)

Circle the meaning associated with each sentence.

EXAMPLE: My keys should be here somewhere.

    a. one of several possibilities

    b. more likely than other possible conclusions

1. I may need to go back to work to look for my keys.

    a. one of several possibilities

    b. the only possible conclusion

2. The keys could be near the copy machine.

    a. more likely than other possible conclusions

    b. one of several possibilities

3. The keys couldn't be lost! I know I didn't lose them.

    a. not a possible conclusion

    b. one of several possibilities

4. I must have left them in the car because you opened the door for me.

    a. one of several possibilities

    b. the only possible conclusion

■ EXERCISE 4   (*Focus 3*)

Change the following passage to the past time frame.

EXAMPLE: Why is Kate so happy? She may get that promotion.

          Why was Kate so happy? She may have gotten that promotion.

(1) Susan is late to the dinner party. **(2)** There may be traffic on the way. **(3)** She could call from her car phone. **(4)** The phone must not be working. **(5)** She must be frustrated.

_____

_____

_____

_____

_____

■ EXERCISE 5   (*Focus 3*)

Write the appropriate perfect modal in each blank. There may be more than one correct answer.

1. Why was Tina crying? She **(A)** _____ (be) upset about the news she received. It was a long-distance call. It **(B)** _____ (be) her son. In his letter he said he was going to come to the graduation party. He **(C)** _____ (arrive) two days ago.

2. What happened? I thought you were going to come to the party. You
(A) _____ (call). Your car? That's no problem. I
(B) _____ (give) you a ride. You **(C)** _____ (have) a
date last night.

3. There's $50 missing from my wallet! Who **(A)** _____ (take) it? I
(B) _____ (left) my wallet in my locker or I
(C) _____ (give) the waiter a $50 tip! I **(D)** _____
(wear) my glasses!

EXERCISE 6   (*Focus 3*)

Complete the crossword puzzle.

ACROSS

  1. You can make predictions and inferences about past events by using _____ modals.
11. A modal of advice.
13. A modal that means "hafta."
15. "In the past, I _____ to take the subway."
16. An empty space where you can fill in a word.
17. A modal that is similar to "may."

DOWN

  1. A time frame that describes an event that is completely over.
  8. A modal that indicates possibility in the past.
12. Without a _____, English would be boring without modals.
14. A short word that means "yes"; sometimes used as a question.

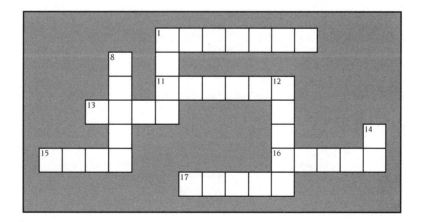

UNIT 17
Hypothetical Statements

EXERCISE 1   (*Focus 1*)

Choose the sentence (a or b) that correctly reflects the implied meaning of each hypothetical statement. Discuss your answers with a partner.

1. You could have gotten a higher grade.

   a. You didn't get a high grade because you didn't study.

   b. You got a higher grade because you studied.

2. I wish you would have called.

   a. You called.

   b. You didn't call.

3. You could have finished on time.

   a. You had the ability to be quicker.

   b. You finished on time.

4. You might at least have put on a clean shirt for the party!

   a. You wore a clean shirt.

   b. You wore a dirty shirt.

5. Dick would have been here earlier, but he got stuck in traffic.

   a. He arrived on time.

   b. He arrived late.

For each hypothetical statement, write the implied meaning. Follow the examples.

EXAMPLES: I would have stayed in school.

I left school.

He could have taken a trip around the world.

He didn't take the trip.

1. I would have lived in Paris for a year.

_____

2. He could have paid his share of the expenses.

_____

3. I would come to your party if I had time.

_____

4. If he needed help, he should have asked me.

_____

5. She could have started the machine if she had thought about it.

_____

6. Bob should have told the truth while he still had the chance.

_____

EXERCISE 3   (*Focus 2*)

Choose the sentence (a or b) that correctly reflects the implied meaning of each statement. Discuss your answers with a partner.

1. If I have the money, I send my mother flowers for Mother's Day.

  a. I always do this.

  b. I do this when I have money.

2. If Cheryl had studied for her exam, I'm sure she would have done quite well.

  a. She didn't study.

  b. She studied.

3. If Bob has to go into the army, he won't be able to finish school.

  a. He may have to go into the army.

  b. He doesn't have to go into the army.

4. If Carl had the energy, he would mow the lawn.

    a. He will mow the lawn.

    b. He won't mow the lawn.

5. If Kate had been at the office, she would have helped you.

    a. Kate helped you.

    b. Kate didn't help you.

EXERCISE 4   (*Focus 3*)

Change these statements of condition and result into hypothetical conditionals.

EXAMPLE: I'm not the president of this country. (condition)

              We pay too many taxes. (result)

              Hypothetical: *If I were the president of this country, we wouldn't pay so many taxes.*

1. I don't have $20,000. I can't afford to pay next year's tuition.

2. My mother isn't here. She doesn't cook for me.

3. The manager is visiting our department. We all have to wear suits.

4. My writing teacher doesn't return essays on time. I don't understand how to improve my writing.

5. Mary has to study. She can't have a part-time job.

6. Alice isn't going to graduate next semester. I don't need a new roommate.

_____

_____

EXERCISE 5 (*Focus 3*)

Here are some hypothetical results. Add hypothetical conditions that are true for you.

EXAMPLE: I would quit my job   _if I had enough money._____

1. Tom would be healthier _____

_____

2. I would make you a cake_____

_____

3. Mary would drive to work _____

_____

4. We wouldn't have to be in this class_____

_____

5. My family would be happier_____

_____

6. I wouldn't have to clean my apartment_____

_____

7. The government wouldn't need an army _____

_____

8. Police wouldn't need to carry guns _____

_____

PART A

Here are some past-tense conditions. Add past-time hypothetical results that are possible answers.

EXAMPLE: If penicillin hadn't been invented, *many more people would have died.*

1. If my grandparents had traveled on the Titanic, _____

_____

2. If Sam had saved his money, _____

_____

3. If I had known you were hungry, _____

_____

4. If Jack hadn't noticed the bomb, _____

_____

PART B

Add present or future time results to the following sentences.

EXAMPLES: If I had been born rich, *I wouldn't be working today.*

If I had been born rich, *I would be taking a vacation next month.*

5. If I had already passed Freshman Writing, _____

_____

6. If my country had more universities, _____

_____

7. If I had gotten a scholarship, _____

_____

8. If off-campus apartments weren't so expensive, _____

_____

Rewrite the following sentences in nonhypothetical language.

EXAMPLE: If I had the time, I would help you fix your car.

I don't have enough time to help you fix your car.

1. I would go back to my country if I didn't have to finish this term paper.

_____

_____

2. I wouldn't have invited him to the party if I had known that he was so impolite.

_____

_____

3. If I had attended this college 20 years ago, I wouldn't be paying such high tuition.

_____

_____

4. If Janice had passed her exam, she wouldn't be retaking the class in summer school.

_____

_____

5. He would have gotten the job if he hadn't lied on his resume.

_____

_____

6. If she had three tickets, she would give you one.

_____

_____

The following are some actual conditions. State a hypothetical result for each using *otherwise* or *but*.

EXAMPLE: I don't know the answer.

I don't know the answer. Otherwise I would tell you.

I would tell you, but I don't know the answer.

1. I had to go to the lab last night.

_____

_____

2. My roommate doesn't know how much I dislike country music.

_____

_____

3. It's going to snow tomorrow.

_____

_____

4. Carol doesn't know how to drive yet.

_____

_____

5. Many people come to the United States for political freedom.

_____

_____

6. Catherine doesn't know how hard Jack is studying.

_____

_____

7. Simon is not the manager of that project.

_____

_____

8. My boss asked me to work this weekend.

_____

_____

PART A

Do the following sentences indicate statements that are likely (actual possibilities) or unlikely (theoretical possibilities)?

EXAMPLES: If I go to the beach, I'll get a tan <u>likely (actual)</u>

If I went to school in Paris, I would study in French. <u>unlikely (theoretical)</u>

1. If Maggie had insurance, she would see the doctor. _____

2. If I get promoted, I'll get a bigger office. _____

3. If you receive another "D," you'll be on academic probation. _____

4. If you had six children, you would need a big house. _____

PART B

Indicate next to each question whether it is hypothetical (not a real situation) or nonhypothetical (it could really happen).

EXAMPLE: Will you ever dye your hair? <u>nonhypothetical</u>

Would you ever take a trip to the moon? <u>hypothetical</u>

5. Would you ever cheat on a test? _____

6. Will he ever learn to stop doing that? _____

7. Will Jane and Bob ever get married? _____

8. Would our teacher ever take a week off and fly to Paris in the middle of the semester?

_____

Do these sentences indicate statements of past possibility or unlikely events that did not happen?

EXAMPLES: I didn't go there, but John might have. _past possibility_

If you had gone, you might have gotten his autograph.

unlikely event

1. You could have negotiated a higher salary when you got the job. _____

2. I didn't taste the lasagna, but Carol may have. _____

3. If Senta had married an American, she would have her green card. _____

4. Peter didn't ask for a receipt, but he could have. _____

EXERCISE 11 (Focus 8)

Decide whether the statement expresses a situation that is not true or one that is an actual possibility.

EXAMPLES: I wish that you liked Mark. _not true_

I hope you liked the party. _actual possibility_

1. Janice wishes that her mother knew how to drive. _____

2. Pat hopes that his raise will show up on his next check. _____

3. I wish that the TOEFL were easier. _____

4. The college hopes that you will all donate money to the alumni fund. _____

5. The manager wishes that he didn't have to fire Tom. _____

Read the following sentences and circle the implied meaning that best matches the meaning of the sentence.

EXAMPLE: Suppose we bought a boat?

a. We will definitely buy a boat.

b. We are just talking about buying a boat.

1. Pretend that you are the teacher. What kind of test would you give?

   a. You are the teacher.

   b. You aren't the teacher.

2. Imagine if you didn't have to work every summer?

   a. You have to work every summer.

   b. You don't have to work every summer.

3. Suppose you took a year off?

   a. You are planning on taking a year off.

   b. Taking a year off is just a dream.

4. Don't pretend to be something that you are not.

   a. You should pretend.

   b. I don't want you to even think about it.

5. I don't suppose that it's possible.

   a. It's not possible.

   b. It is possible.

UNIT 18

Sensory Verbs, Causative Verbs, and Verbs that Take Subjunctive

EXERCISE 1 (Focus 1)

Underline the base verb form or participle that comes after the highlighted verbs in the following story. The first two sentences have been done for you.

Last night I **heard** a cat <u>meowing</u> outside my door. My curiosity **made** me <u>get up</u> and <u>go</u> to the window. To my surprise I saw a tiny wet kitten scratching on the door. It **demanded** to be let in.

I **let** the cat into the kitchen and dried it off. I **allowed** it to sit on a chair. I made some warm milk for the kitten and **forced** the kitten to finish all of it.

After all this, the kitten **insisted** that she be let back outside.

EXERCISE 2 (Focus 2)

Identify the sensory verb in each of the following sentences. Restate the observed action as a separate sentence.

EXAMPLE: I saw the cat kill the rat.

Sensory verb: saw

Observed action: <u>The cat killed the rat.</u>

1. We watched the children skating on the lake.

Sensory verb: _____

Observed action: _____

2. Carol likes to feel the sun on her face.

Sensory verb: _____

Observed action: _____

3. Charles heard the car crash.

Sensory verb: _____

Observed action: _____

4. Pat observed the baby crawling on the floor.

Sensory verb: _____

Observed action: _____

5. I smell the toast burning.

Sensory verb: _____

Observed action: _____

6. The manager listened to the customer complain about the broken washing machine.

Sensory verb: _____

Observed action: _____

EXERCISE 3 (Focus 2)

Decide on which verb form to use based on the context and underline it. In some sentences, both forms may be possible. Discuss this with a partner.

EXAMPLE: On my way to school, I saw Jack (ride/<u>riding</u>) his motorcycle.

1. I watched the kitten (play/playing) with the string.

2. As Susan watched the mechanic (fix/fixing) her old car, she decided to get a new one.

3. I heard the gardener (mow/mowing) the lawn so I went outside to talk to him.

4. Pat saw Mary (leave/leaving) so he ran to catch her.

5. Janice smelled something (burn/burning) so she called the fire department.

EXERCISE 4 (Focus 2)

Restate the numbered sentences in the paragraph as sensory verb complements.

EXAMPLE: Here is what Betty saw: **(1)** Two children were playing in the sandbox. **(2)** They were laughing and shouting. **(3)** One child hit the other child. **(4)** That child screamed in pain.

(1) Betty saw two children playing in the sandbox. **(2)** She heard them laughing and shouting. **(3)** She watched one child hit the other child. **(4)** She heard that child scream in pain.

Here is what I heard, saw, and felt during an earthquake: **(1)** The house began to shake. **(2)** The sound of the movement got louder. **(3)** The dishes fell out of the kitchen cabinet. **(4)** There was a sound of breaking glass. **(5)** I went under a table. **(6)** The sound grew fainter.

_____

_____

_____

_____

_____

_____

EXERCISE 5 (Focus 2)

Choose the correct form of each verb given. In some cases, both answers may be correct. Discuss this with a partner.

1. As the earthquake grew stronger, I heard the dishes (fall/falling) out of the cabinet and (break/breaking) on the floor.

2. The manager caught the employee (steal/stealing) the cash.

3. The children watched the dog (bite/biting) the postal carrier.

4. I smell something (burn/burning). Is the neighbor cooking again?

5. We discovered the children (play/playing) with matches.

6. Kate heard Carl (argue/arguing) with his cousin.

Underline each causative verb and circle the infinitive or base form of the verb that follows. One sentence has been done for you.

(1) Patrick started a new job last week. **(2)** When he arrived, his boss <u>had</u> him (sit) next to the bill collector. **(3)** The bill collector made Patrick dial all of his phone calls. **(4)** Then the bill collector forced Patrick to listen. **(5)** He made the people say they would pay.

(6) The next day, Patrick worked with the secretary. **(7)** She got Patrick to file all of her correspondence. **(8)** She also made him photocopy old letters. **(9)** Later Patrick helped the secretary organize the files.

(10) On the third day, the boss let Patrick start his real job now that he understood the jobs of others in the office.

EXERCISE 7   *(Focus 3)*

For each statement of causer/doer/action listed, choose an appropriate causative that expresses your opinion. Write two complete sentences expressing that opinion: one with a causative verb and one with a verb and infinitive complement.

EXAMPLE: *Causer:* parents

Doer: children

Action: clean their rooms

Causative: <u>Parents should make children clean their rooms.</u>

Verb and infinitive: <u>Parents should require children to clean their rooms.</u>

1. Causer: cat owners / Doer: cats / Action: scratch guests

   _____

   _____

2. Causer: teachers / Doer: students / Action: type term papers

   _____

   _____

3. Causer: thief / Doer: victim / Action: give up his watch

   _____

   _____

4. Causer: schools / Doer: doctors / Action: examine students once a year

_____

_____

5. Causer: teachers / Doer: students / Action: learn by example

_____

_____

6. Causer: doctor / Doer: Jack / Action: go on a diet

_____

_____

7. Causer: most people / Doer: an accountant / Action: to check their taxes

_____

_____

8. Causer: police officers / Doer: drunk drivers / Action: to pull over

_____

_____

_____

EXERCISE 8   **(Focus 4)**

Decide whether the causative verbs in these sentences can be made passive without losing information or being ungrammatical. If so, write the passive version of the sentence.

EXAMPLES: The city government requires all drivers to have car insurance.

All drivers are required to have car insurance.

The mother got her child to clean his room.

No change possible.

1. The law doesn't allow people to drink and drive.

_____

_____

2. We got the plumber to come right over.

_____

_____

3. The government requires all adult men to enlist in the army.

_____

_____

4. We let the attendant take our coats.

_____

_____

5. Wilson had his sister prepare his report.

_____

_____

6. Parents should help their children learn good eating habits.

_____

_____

EXERCISE 9   (Focus 4)

Restate all the passive causatives in this paragraph as active constructions. Use _boss_ as a probable agent. Sentence 1 has been done for you as an example.

EXAMPLE: _The boss required him to answer the phones for several hours._

Patrick's fifth day on the job was better than the first four. **(1)** He was required to answer the phone for several hours. **(2)** When the phones were slow, Patrick was allowed to read the reports from the past month. **(3)** Later, he was taught to use the fax machine. **(4)** When it was noon, Patrick was allowed to go out to lunch. **(5)** But he was required to bring back lunch for several people on the phone staff. **(6)** Patrick had been persuaded to pick up a newspaper and some rubber bands as well. **(7)** At 5:00, Patrick was encouraged to work a few minutes extra. **(8)** At 6:30, Patrick was allowed to go home.

_____

_____

_____

_____

_____

_____

_____

_____

_____

_____

_____

_____

EXERCISE 10 *(Focus 5)*

     Decide whether each sentence is correct or incorrect. In the incorrect sentences, identify the mistake and fix it.

1. The children were gotten to be quiet. _____

2. The professor made the students to redo their chemistry experiments. _____

3. He encouraged all of his students to be careful. _____

4. The man has his suit to be tailored. _____

5. I had the landlord be fix the leaky faucet. _____

6. Tom persuaded his parents to let him take flying lessons. _____

7. He let his roommate to borrow his best suit. _____

8. A mechanic was had to change the oil. _____

9. The police department requires that every officer on the street carries a gun. _____

10. My instructor made me to write my term paper. _____

11. My grandmother demanded that she was included in our travel plans. _____

12. Bambang requested that he was given a break. _____

Choose the *one* word or phrase that best completes each sentence.

1. On the third Monday of each April, thousands of people line a 26.2-mile road from Hopkinton to Boston, Massachusetts, to watch nearly 10,000 athletes _____ the Boston Marathon.

    (A) run

    (B) to run

    (C) running

    (D) are running

2. Yesterday, Rita's voice sounded fully recovered, so she _____ be able to sing at tonight's performance.

    (A) must

    (B) might

    (C) should

    (D) won't

3. If you _____ what she is going through, you wouldn't be so critical.

    (A) know

    (B) knew

    (C) had known

    (D) would know

4. The immigration official had Vijak _____ an immigration entry card upon his arrival in the United States.

    (A) to fill out

    (B) fill out

    (C) filling out

    (D) filled out

5. If Anna hadn't kept a detailed record of all the expenditures, we _____ where all the money went.

    (A) might have known

    (B) might

    (C) would have known

    (D) wouldn't know

6. To be on the safe side, we should fill up the tank now because we _____ run out of gas on the way.

    (A) must

    (B) might

    (C) will

    (D) should

7. Many people believe that the rich should be _____ pay higher taxes.

    (A) gotten to

    (B) required

    (C) made to

    (D) let

8. We _____ to a Broadway show in New York, but our visit was so short, and we had so many things to see.

(A) would go
(B) should be going
(C) would have gone
(D) couldn't have gone

9. Michael called and we chatted, but he didn't congratulate me, so he _____ heard about my promotion.

(A) shouldn't have
(B) will have
(C) might have
(D) must not have

10. I wish I _____ my education so I would have a better job now.

(A) finished
(B) had finished
(C) can finish
(D) would finish

Identify the *one* underlined word or phrase that must be changed for the sentence to be grammatically correct.

11. If you <u>heard</u> her <u>speak</u> English, you <u>would have</u> sworn she <u>was</u> a native speaker.
          A   **B**   **C**   **D**

12. We <u>wish</u> Elias <u>could have</u> spent more time with us because we <u>could enjoy</u> listening to
      A   **B**   **C**
him <u>tell</u> more stories of his trip around the world.
    D

13. After many years as a football talent scout, Gregory <u>must</u> get very tired and <u>may</u> be
                                         A   **B**
endangering his health if he <u>would have to</u> travel around the country all the time
                            C
watching college players <u>play football</u>.
                D

14. If the doctors <u>had detected</u> the tumor earlier and if the operation <u>was</u> successful, perhaps
                A   **B**
the cancer <u>would</u> not have spread, and Gina <u>might</u> still be alive today.
          C   **D**

15. Diana wanted to look especially nice for <u>the</u> senior prom; so she bought <u>a</u> new dress, she
                                A   **B**
got her hair <u>to be done</u>, and then she and her date had their picture <u>taken</u>.
          C   **D**

16. When the police <u>wished</u> to ask George who he saw <u>stole</u> his car, he <u>shouldn't have</u> <u>had to</u>
               A   **B**   **C**   **D**
go down to the police station.

17. <u>Were I born</u> in America 500 years ago, I <u>would have been</u> one of the Native Americans; I
      A   **B**

<u>might have been</u> a Navajo, a Chippewa, a Sioux, or an Eskimo, and I <u>could have had</u> a
    C   **D**

name like Eagle Eye or Dances With Wolves.

18. If I <u>were</u> tall and <u>could play</u> basketball superbly, I <u>would have wanted</u> to play for the
      A   **B**   **C**

Chicago Bulls and <u>be</u> famous like Michael Jordan.
                 D

19. Amanda wishes she <u>could have known</u> her grandparents when they <u>were</u> young, because
                   A   **B**

they <u>must have been</u> so lively and charming and because she and they <u>would feel</u> instant
    C   **D**

closeness at that earlier time.

20. If Matthew <u>were to</u> choose another era to live in, he <u>would probably pick</u> Vienna at the
              A   **B**

turn of the century, just so he <u>can hear</u> Gustav Mahler <u>conduct</u> the Vienna Opera.
                             C   **D**

UNIT

19 Articles in Discourse

EXERCISE 1 (*Focus 1*)

Identify and underline the determiners in these sentences. Are they demonstratives, possessives, quantifiers, or articles? Follow the example.

EXAMPLE: <u>The</u> cut on <u>his</u> arm will take <u>some</u> time to heal.
article   possessive   article

1. The man who lives next door broke his glasses.

2. The university has some new requirements.

3. That song is about the Civil War.

4. Few people ate the fried liver.

5. Those gifts are for her graduation party.

6. Much has been said about their problem with the law.

EXERCISE 2 (*Focus 3*)

Decide whether the highlighted noun phrases in these sentences are generic (refer to classes or categories) or particular (refer to members of a class).

EXAMPLES: **The blue chairs** are on sale at Bloomingdale's. ___*particular*___

Chairs should be comfortable to sit in. ___*generic*___

1. **A college** needs to have a good cafeteria.

    _____

2. **Some people** will come over tonight for

    dessert. _____

3. **Cheetahs** are the fastest land animals.

    _____

DUANE GILLOGLY

4. The cheetah in the local zoo is 12 years old. _____

5. They went looking for **a new car** yesterday. _____

6. Many students don't like long classes. _____

7. Students taking lab classes spend a lot of time on campus. _____

8. A wet cat is an unhappy cat. _____

9. Books for the new library were donated by the Alumni Association.

_____

10. There weren't **many students** in the library this weekend. _____

EXERCISE 3 (*Focus 4*)

Choose the correct implication for each of these sentences. ("I" refers to the speaker or writer. "You" refers to the listener or reader.)

1. Let's see a movie tonight.

   a. We have already decided which movie to see.

   b. Let's choose a movie.

2. Please give me a red pen.

   a. Any red pen would be fine.

   b. I have a specific red pen in mind.

3. You have some reports to show me, don't you?

   a. I'm sure that you have these reports.

   b. I don't know whether you have these reports or not.

4. We should bring a gift to the party.

   a. You have a specific gift in mind.

   b. You haven't decided what to get.

5. Did your teacher say anything about exams?

   a. I am asking about any exam.

   b. I am asking about a specific exam.

Decide whether these sentences require definite or indefinite articles. Add the appropriate article (*a, an, the, some,* or Ø) in each blank. There may be more than one correct answer.

1. Jackie brought _____ coffee for the office meeting.

2. Mark wants to buy _____ new car, so he is out looking today.

3. Did you give _____ waiter his pen back? I think he's looking for it.

4. The Smiths have _____ financial problems that they don't want the bank to know about.

5. _____ store that has televisions on sale is also offering _____ $10.00 rebate.

6. Although it was _____ nice party, I spent most of my time in _____ kitchen.

7. _____ salesman came by to talk to you. I think he was from a supply company.

8. Carla was treated by _____ doctor in _____ emergency room.

9. Susan didn't find _____ computer program that she was looking for.

10. Would you like _____ salt with your meal?

EXERCISE 5   (*Focus 5*)

Write the correct articles (*a, an, Ø, some,* or *the*) in each blank. More than one answer may be correct.

1. I saw **(A)** _____ movie this weekend in **(B)** _____ college theater. **(C)** _____ movie was three hours long and most of **(D)** _____ people in **(E)** _____ audience left before it was over. **(F)** _____ people were quiet when they left, but others were noisy and **(G)** _____ manager had to be called in.

2. **(A)** _____ students don't realize when they should begin **(B)** _____ term paper. When should they start **(C)** _____ note cards? How many times should they visit **(D)** _____ library? **(E)** _____ term paper is a very important part of **(F)** _____ student's grade.

3. Louise doesn't like **(A)** _____ ham. Whenever she goes to **(B)** _____ party, she asks **(C)** _____ hostess what will be served for **(D)** _____ dinner. **(E)** _____ people think her behavior is rude.

Add the correct article (*a, an, some* or Ø) to each blank in the following sentences. **More than one answer may be correct.**

1. I once took _____ class for which every student had to take _____ lab.

2. Carl visited _____ castles in France, Italy, and England.

3. Mr. Southland is _____ very fair instructor and _____ very nice person.

4. There is _____ new car in _____ parking space next to mine.

5. _____ teachers don't give much homework.

6. Jack is _____ musician in _____ band downtown.

7. There is _____ purple tree in _____ park somewhere with my name carved in it.

8. Mark took _____ long time even though it was _____ easy test.

9. I once had _____ cat whose name was Tiger. It was _____ good cat, but it liked to sit on my books.

10. He's _____ selfish guy and he doesn't like to spend _____ money.

Write the appropriate article (*a, an, the*, or Ø) in each blank. **There may be more than one correct answer. Pay special attention to unfamiliar nouns.**

1. We want to buy _____ bracelet that she liked for her birthday.

2. Before we leave on vacation, let's ask _____ neighbors to water _____ plants.

3. Is there _____ radio in _____ kitchen?

4. _____ meat that we bought yesterday is too tough to eat.

5. Please make _____ extra key for _____ front door.

6. Tomorrow there will be _____ lecture on _____ history of Canada.

7. When my brother asked me how I had done on _____ exam, all I could do was look up at _____ sky.

8. Have you enjoyed _____ out-of-town basketball games that you've gone to?

9. We were sitting in _____ auditorium talking about _____ assignment that we had just turned in.

10. _____ first time I ever went swimming, I jumped off _____ diving board.

11. I'll meet you at _____ pool after lunch.

12. Whenever _____ friend does something special for me, I usually call or send _____ thank-you card.

EXERCISE 8　(Focus 7)

Decide which answer best matches the meaning of each statement.

1. A busy child is a good child.

   a. This refers to a specific child.

   b. This refers to children in general.

2. Let's go to the pool tomorrow.

   a. We know which pool the speaker is referring to.

   b. This could be any pool.

3. I think you should see a doctor.

   a. I have a specific doctor in mind.

   b. Any doctor can help you. Just make an appointment.

4. Let's go to a restaurant near the beach.

   a. You have a specific restaurant in mind.

   b. It could be any restaurant near the beach.

UNIT
20 Demonstratives in Discourse

EXERCISE 1 (*Focus 1*)

Add the appropriate demonstrative, pronoun, or determiner to each blank. **More than one answer may be possible.**

1. _____ bananas are ripe, but _____ aren't ready for you to eat.

2. Where did you get _____ cookies? _____ taste homemade.

3. After John went to speak to his advisor, Dr. Palmer, he realized that he could only take _____ classes that were marked on his study list.

4. Which of _____ two cars do you like better, _____ small one with the new tires or _____ older one with the good radio?

5. Last summer we went to Alaska and hiked. _____ mountains are much higher than _____ ones in my home state.

6. Where did you get _____ camera? _____ really nice. _____ looks like _____ one my mother has.

7. Carl got a new suit for work. _____ is made of wool. I'm glad he bought _____ suit instead of _____ cotton one he was thinking of buying. _____ is really much nicer.

8. Our engineering professor told us to forget _____ old specifications we had learned and she asked us to learn _____ new ones.

Circle the demonstratives in these sentences. Then draw an arrow indicating what each one refers to. The first sentence has been done for you as an example.

1. Many people left the play early. (This) made the actors angry.

2. Let me make this clear: No cheating!

3. These students are excused from the final exam: Robert Gonzales, Hosein Arifipour, and Carla Arnold.

4. The manager stated that he had received several expense reports that were not filled out correctly. These will be returned.

5. Louise said that she left her job because she wanted more free time. That doesn't sound correct to me.

6. These practices will be stopped immediately: Taking long lunch breaks and leaving early.

7. Smith will write the report and Wilson will wordprocess it. Those are your assignments.

8. Our salaries will be reduced 5 percent. I don't like that.

Add *this*, *that*, or *it* to the blanks in the following sentences. Some sentences can use all three; for some sentences, one form may not be acceptable. Discuss this with a partner.

1. You said "14." Don't you mean "40"? Oh yes, _____ 's what I meant to say.

2. I love the clean air in this city. _____ is why I moved here.

3. Don't worry about the cost of the phone call. _____ really doesn't matter.

4. Dr. Labeque has just announced his resignation. _____ is why I called you to come to this meeting.

5. Patrick's dog was hurt by a car. I thought _____ might happen. He's always leaving the back gate open.

6. Charles left the money on the table? I don't believe _____!

7. I think you should finish your degree. If you drop out of school, you'll regret _____ in the future.

8. Don't tell me about it. _____ is why he's the supervisor.

Identify the demonstratives that are followed by postmodifiers in these sentences. Write "PM" next to those sentences that contain this structure.

1. Compare your essay to that of your partner. _____

2. Carl heard about that job in the employment office. _____

3. Those who cannot hear the difference between "t" and "th" will have trouble on the pronunciation test. _____

4. He put those in the story. _____

5. The teacher only gives As to those she thinks know the material. _____

6. One must learn to tell the difference between that which is genuine and that which is not. _____

Choose the *one* word or phrase that best completes each sentence.

1. Few people ate _____ spinach ravioli.
   - (A) a
   - (B) some
   - (C) the
   - (D) this

2. Melinda, you must be sure to come to my party because there is _____ that I want you to meet.
   - (A) the friend
   - (B) some friends
   - (C) my friend
   - (D) a friend of mine

3. When I heard the gossip about you, I said "_____ the most ridiculous thing I've ever heard."
   - (A) It's
   - (B) This is
   - (C) That's
   - (D) Is

4. Pregnant women are said to eat _____ pickles when they are hungry.
   - (A) any
   - (B) the
   - (C) some
   - (D) Ø (nothing)

5. At the shop, they wanted to show me all the dresses, but I was only interested in _____ in the window.
   - (A) that
   - (B) the one
   - (C) it
   - (D) this

6. We saw a movie with great cinematography and excellent acting, but _____ screenplay left much to be desired.
   - (A) a
   - (B) some
   - (C) this
   - (D) the

7. In the middle of the night I heard a terrifying sound; I called the police immediately because _____ sound was coming from our basement.
   - (A) the
   - (B) a
   - (C) any
   - (D) Ø (nothing)

8. Which of _____ two skirts do you like better?
   - (A) this
   - (B) these
   - (C) that
   - (D) Ø (nothing)

9. "Ray, listen, you're brilliant at what you do, but you're very slow in doing your work, and frankly, _____ what's holding up your career."
   (A) it's   (C) that's
   (B) these   (D) those

10. Gloria is an unusually patient person, but the one thing she can't stand is _____ people who talk compulsively and never let her get a word in edgewise.
    (A) the   (C) some
    (B) Ø (nothing)   (D) that

Identify the *one* underlined word or phrase that must be changed for the sentence to be grammatically correct.

11. <u>Time</u> has come <u>to let</u> management <u>know</u> how we feel and <u>to make</u> them listen to our
      A   B   C   D
    demands.

12. <u>It's</u> surprising to me that <u>the</u> United Nations has <u>the</u> post office that issues its own
     A   B   C
    stamps for the 23,000 UN staff members scattered around <u>the</u> world.
                                                              D

13. I'll <u>let you go</u> because I know you're busy, but let me ask you <u>one</u> last thing: Where did
         A   B
    you buy <u>that</u> ice cream you served us <u>another</u> night?
            C   D

14. Maria wishes she had <u>some</u> seafood to add to her paella dish, but <u>the</u> fresh seafood is
                           A   B
    hard to find, so she'll just put <u>chicken</u> in with <u>the</u> rice, vegetables, saffron, and other
                                       C   D
    seasonings.

15. Sanghee feels somewhat lost when <u>the</u> students in his dorm discuss <u>baseball</u> and <u>other</u>
                                     A   B   C
    sports that <u>the</u> Americans love.
             D

16. We heard on <u>the</u> news that, according to official sources, <u>The</u> president is in perfect
                A   B
    health, but that <u>they</u> with inside information know that <u>that</u> is not entirely true.
                   C   D

17. The coach knows that for his team to win he has to get <u>the</u> players <u>improve</u> on defense
                                                       A   B
    and he has to make them <u>play</u> more aggressively, or else the results will always be <u>the</u>
                              C   D
    same.

18. Bill and Rosaura want to live in <u>the</u> country, where <u>the</u> air is fresh, <u>the</u> water is clean, and
                                            A   **B**   **C**

  <u>the</u> nature is all around them.
  D

19. <u>The</u> glass is <u>a</u> hard, brittle, transparent material that is made from <u>sand</u> melted under
  A   **B**   **C**

  <u>great heat</u>.
      D

20. Gail says that <u>its</u> strange that <u>the</u> phone <u>hasn't rung</u> in <u>a</u> month.
                        A   **B**   **C**   **D**

UNIT

21 Possessives

EXERCISE 1   (Focus 1)

Underline and identify the possessive structures in the following passage. Is each (a) a possessive determiner, (b) a possessive pronoun, (c) a possessive noun, or (d) a possessive phrase? The first two sentences have been done for you as examples.

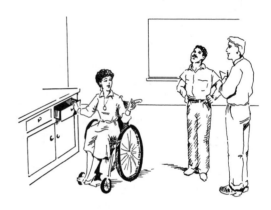

(1) Last week, Anita and Jerry went looking for <u>their</u> first house. (2) <u>Jerry's</u> cousin is a real estate agent. (3) He took them to see his new list of houses for sale. (4) First, he showed them pictures of each house. (5) Then he took them to see each house on his list. (6) Their reactions were mixed. (7) Jerry liked the garden of the condo while Anita liked the kitchen of the last place they visited. (8) At the end of the day, Jerry's feet were tired and Anita's patience was gone. (9) Their enthusiasm for househunting was replaced by a desire to return to a house that was already theirs.

EXERCISE 2   (Focus 2)

For each noun and possessive listed here, write the best possessive form in the blank. Add articles where necessary.

EXAMPLES: profits/business

The profits of the business were reinvested in the business.

whiskers/cat

The cat's whiskers were long and white.

1. golf clubs/friend/Bob

   We borrowed _____

2. symphonies/Beethoven:

_____ are performed all over the world.

3. child/mouth

They found the button they were looking for _____

4. friend Sally/child

Bill gave the baseball to _____

5. first page/book

_____ is often the hardest to write.

6. parking lot/mall

Mark asked me to meet him in the _____

7. son/well-known French movie director

Carla had dinner with _____

8. seat/chair

Michael broke _____ when he stepped on it.

9. store/Susan's cousin

I bought that birthday gift at _____

10. cause/dispute

_____ was the dog's bad habit.

EXERCISE 3 **(Focus 2)**
_____

With a partner, take turns using the possessive to describe people and things in your class, your family, your apartment building, and so on. Write five on a separate piece of paper.

EXAMPLE: *George's new pants are very nice.*

The bathroom on the third floor is always locked.

My cousin's children all have red hair.

EXERCISE 4 (*Focus 3*)

Underline the possessive forms in the following sentences and identify the meaning of each. Do they indicate:

        (a) an amount or quantity
        (b) a part of a whole
        (c) a general relationship/association
        (d) an origin or agent
        (e) actual possession

                      (a)
    EXAMPLE: He gave me <u>five dollars'</u> worth of cheese for four dollars.

  1. The cause of the common cold is still unknown.

  2. Karen's dog is in the back of the store.

  3. We studied the theories of Freud in Professor Randolph's classroom.

  4. The cheeses of Holland are famous for their quality.

  5. Mr. Tuttobene told us of his hikes in the wilderness of Yosemite.

  6. The author revealed the killer in the book's last two pages.

EXERCISE 5 (*Focus 3*)

Are the following sentences correct ("C") or incorrect ("I")? If they are incorrect, identify the problem and correct it.

    EXAMPLE: The lawyer's investigation's results show that his client is innocent. <u> I </u>

              <u>The results of the lawyer's investigation show that his client is innocent.</u>

  1. The house's roof was damaged in the storm.

_____

_____

  2. George's son's business is doing well.

_____

_____

  3. He was his own fame's prisoner when he died.

_____

_____

4. England's wool sweaters are famous for their quality.

_____

_____

5. Victoria's sister is leaving for a three-day vacation.

_____

_____

6. A little-known singer's wife's stepdaughter will be playing the guitar tomorrow night.

_____

_____

UNIT

22 Quantifiers and Collective Nouns

In the following passage underline the quantifiers and the noun phrases they modify. The first sentence has been done for you.

(1) <u>Many students</u> apply to <u>several colleges</u> to be sure that they will be accepted by at least one. (2) There are plenty of colleges to choose from, but not all of them offer every major field of study. (3) For this reason, quite a few students start their studies at one college and then transfer to another. (4) Most students have to decide on or "declare" a major by the third year of school.

(5) Almost all schools have counselors who can offer some assistance to students who can't decide on a major. (6) Many counseling departments require students to take a test to determine their interests. (7) Hardly anyone refuses, since these tests are free. (8) Quite a bit of the counselors' advice is guesswork. (9) More than one counselor told me that I should teach business or become a lawyer, but I enjoy teaching ESL (most of the time).

(10) Not many students are fortunate enough to discover their majors right away. (11) A lot of students take three or four courses in one area and then realize that the major isn't right for them. (12) Some people then have to take their hardest courses in their last year of school. (13) A few unlucky students have to return for a fifth year of school to complete their degree.

Change the following statements concerning number or amount to sentences using quantifiers.

EXAMPLE: I'm having a great amount of trouble finding the right birthday present for Sheila.

I'm having a lot of trouble finding the right birthday present for Sheila.

1. There are a small number of cookies left in the jar.

_____

_____

2. The vast majority of parents worry about their children.

_____

_____

3. An unspecified number of teachers work in the summer.

_____

_____

4. The majority of homeowners in the United States have some kind of homeowner's insurance.

_____

_____

5. The total number of children in the United States must have vaccinations before they may start school.

_____

_____

6. It takes a large amount of money to buy a house.

_____

_____

EXERCISE 3   (Focus 2)

With a partner, write sentences on a separate piece of paper using the quantifiers listed below. Describe education in your country or describe the types of jobs that people have in different regions of your country.

EXAMPLE: most   Most women in the United States have to work outside the home.

1. all	7. some
2. a great many	8. any
3. quite a few	9. a few
4. a lot of	10. a great deal of
5. a little	11. much
6. several	12. a little

EXERCISE 4   (Focus 2)

Decide whether to use *few* or *a few*, *little* or *a little*. Compare your answers to those of a partner.

1. Jack had _____ respect for those who cheated on the exam.

2. There's _____ coffee left. Do you want it?

3. Sam was very poor as a child. As a result, he had _____ advantages.

4. Can I meet with you after class? I'm having _____ trouble with these algebra problems.

5. The average American child had _____ cavities during childhood. I suppose it's because American children eat so much candy.

6. He spent so much money on his vacation that there's _____ money left to pay the rent.

7. _____ wives would be as understanding as Joan.

8. There's _____ bit of hot water left. Go ahead and take a shower.

EXERCISE 5 (Focus 3)

Change the following statements with plural count nouns to statements with *any*, *each*, or *every*. Remember to make any other necessary changes to preserve the original meaning of the sentence. More than one answer may be correct.

EXAMPLE: All animals have a basic instinct for survival.

Every animal has a basic instinct for survival.

Any animal has a basic instinct for survival.

1. All students want to get a good grade.

_____

_____

2. All postal carriers were warned about dogs.

_____

_____

3. Jack spends all his paychecks on his car.

_____

_____

4. All letters will be answered.

_____

_____

EXERCISE 6 (Focus 3)

Choose among the quantifiers *both, neither, either, both of them,* and *either of them* to be used in the following sentences.

1. _____ children went to the baseball game.

2. _____ ate hot dogs and peanuts.

3. _____ wants to leave the game early.

4. Christine likes_____ job offers. She will accept _____ offer.

5. Paul has applied for two loans. He will accept _____.

EXERCISE 7 (Focus 4)

Decide whether to use the quantifier in parentheses alone or with *of* in the following sentences.

1. (Some) _____ neighbors in my apartment building have pets.

2. (Any) _____ cashier can assist you.

3. (A little) _____ the money that Horace earned last summer is still left.

4. (No/None) _____ checks are accepted.

5. (Almost all) _____ young children require naps.

6. (Most) _____ department stores accept credit cards.

7. There's (hardly any) _____ sugar left in the bowl.

8. (Several) _____ books that I lost turned up in the lost and found office.

EXERCISE 8 (Focus 5)

Choose the correct form of the words in parentheses in the following sentences.

1. Hardly any students (attended/didn't attend) the rally.

2. Bob had to count (every/every one) before he closed the box.

3. Is it true that no money was collected at the fundraiser? Yes, (none/no) was.

4. Do you have (many/every/much) time to finish?

5. No problem. I have (lots /a lot).

6. Many students apply for scholarships, but only (not many/a few) get them.

7. Paul will need (any/none of/a great deal of) persistence.

8. Can every student get a library card? Yes, (each/every one) can.

EXERCISE 9 (Focus 6)

Read the following passages, underlining the words and phrases that refer to groups or categories of nouns. The first passage has been done for you as an example.

1. Anne and Jerry were quite upset when they returned from their vacation. Not only was there <u>a bundle of bills</u> waiting for them, but their garden looked like <u>a pack of wild dogs</u> had been living there for a week. All of the lawn chairs were overturned and there were paper plates and cups everywhere. Their <u>condominium association</u> had used their garden for a meeting, but they didn't put the chairs away or cover the garbage cans.

2. Toshi went with some friends to visit an American zoo. He was surprised to see so many animals in such large groups. He saw a flock of pink birds…flamingos they were called. Then he saw a gaggle of geese…these birds made a lot of noise. There was a herd of goats next to a flock of sheep. When Toshi and his friends sat down to have lunch, they were surrounded by a swarm of bees who wanted their sugary soda!

3. A committee of professors will be sent to Switzerland to study the effects of noise pollution on herds of dairy cows. The professors will be escorted around several farms by a delegation of dairy farmers.

4. Both the government and the public have been angry with the media's presentation of election results. A group of unhappy citizens met with a team of media analysts to discuss what they considered to be unfair reporting practices.

EXERCISE 10 *(Focus 6)*

Decide whether you should use the collective nouns in the following sentences with singular or plural verbs and pronouns and choose the correct form. Although both choices may be grammatically correct, there may be a clear preference for one form instead of the other. With your partner, discuss why you have chosen one form over the other.

1. The committee of government agents (has/have) released (their/its) decision to the media.
2. The team (is/are) practicing (its/their) routines and moves before the game.
3. The media (are/is) responsible for (their/its) action in reporting the news.
4. The staff voted to take (its/their) vacations consecutively.
5. The middle class (is/are) unhappy and are showing (its/their) dissatisfaction in (its/their) voting.

EXERCISE 11 *(Focus 6)*

Decide whether the proper nouns in the following sentences are treated as singular or plural. Choose the verbs and pronouns in parentheses accordingly.

1. The French usually (drinks/drink) wine with (its/their) main meals.
2. The Supreme Court (have/has) decided to change (their/its) position on that matter.
3. The Catholic Church (have/has) closed many schools in (its/their) poorer parishes.
4. The Brooklyn Dodgers (was/were) moved to Los Angeles about 30 years ago.

5. The government of China (has/have) made it impossible for (its/their) people to have large families.

6. The Wilsons (is/are) going to take (its/their) vacation in Nova Scotia this year.

EXERCISE 12 (Focus 7)

For each *the + adjective* construction in the following sentences, rewrite the construction as *noun + relative clause.*

EXAMPLE: The media didn't protect the privacy of the victims.

The victims = the people who were hurt or used.

The media didn't protect the privacy of the people who were hurt or used.

1. Fast bicycles and large pizzas are very popular with the young.

_____

_____

2. Very few well-paying jobs are open to the illiterate.

_____

_____

3. The shelters were opened to prevent the homeless from dying.

_____

_____

4. Some hospitals in the United States specialize in diseases of the elderly.

_____

_____

5. Porsches and Ferraris are generally considered to be cars for the rich.

_____

_____

Choose the *one* word or phrase that best completes each sentence.

1. During _____, many doctors are on vacation, so it's hard to get regular medical care.
   - (A) August's month
   - (B) the August month
   - (C) the month of August
   - (D) the month of August's

2. In general, _____ to be opposed to new taxes.
   - (A) the public seems
   - (B) the public seem
   - (C) a public seems
   - (D) the publics seem

3. I'm afraid _____ of the volunteers here tonight won't be able to answer your questions, so perhaps you should ask the supervisor.
   - (A) any
   - (B) all
   - (C) not all
   - (D) many

4. Professor Warner is not my colleague but _____.
   - (A) a colleague of Peter
   - (B) a colleague of Peter's
   - (C) a Peter's colleague
   - (D) the colleague from Peter

5. _____ difficulty that students have with the schedule is with the early morning classes.
   - (A) Much
   - (B) Plenty of
   - (C) Much of the
   - (D) A great many

6. Your research team has made tremendous progress toward its goal, but you need to do _____ more work before you can publish your findings.
   - (A) a few
   - (B) few
   - (C) little
   - (D) a little

7. The crew _____ for their success in landing the disabled aircraft safely.
   - (A) praised
   - (B) was praised
   - (C) were praised
   - (D) is praising

8. Dr. Kimble's new office is located right next to _____.
   - (A) the office of Jeff's great ear, nose, and throat doctor
   - (B) Jeff's great ear, nose, and throat doctor's office
   - (C) the office of the great ear, nose, and throat doctor of Jeff
   - (D) the great ear, nose, and throat doctor's office of Jeff

9. _____ employees are allowed to use the company day-care center.
    (A) Each   (C) Any
    (B) Every   (D) All

10. The Boston Red Sox _____ a longstanding rivalry with the New York Yankees.
    (A) has had   (C) are
    (B) have had   (D) is

Identify the *one* underlined word or phrase that must be changed for the sentence to be grammatically correct.

11. Hardly any of the staff in the registrar's office is coming to work the day before
    A   **B**   **C**   **D**
Thanksgiving.

12. The building management has decided that there will be no security guards after
        A   **B**   **C**
midnight, which is precisely when we need a great deal of them.
                                   D

13. A few of our visitors know we have the doorbell by the side entrance to our house, but
    A   **B**
most of them just use the front door's knocker.
    C   **D**

14. When Linda got a new apartment, like most renters, she had to pay an incredible lot of
                        A   **B**
money: the realtor's fee, a security deposit, and two months' rent.
          C   **D**

15. Like the earth's orbit, Mars's orbit is almost circular, but it is somewhat more off center
          A   **B**
than the orbits of many of the other planets.
     C   **D**

16. Nowadays each of the winner of the Nobel Prize also wins a cash award of approximately
              A   **B**   **C**   **D**
$1.2 million.

17. Almost none of the software produced by that company is really useful for the
       A   **B**
general public or the inexperienceds.
    C   **D**

18. The University of Michigan's team was proud of its victory over ours, but actually,
       A   **B**   **C**
neither team played very well.
    D

19. A good number of talent has gone into creating this production of "Phantom of
        A   **B**

the Opera," and any audience would be impressed by it, but to me several key performers
                C   **D**

just weren't good enough as singers.

20. I would prefer a little of your white wine, but actually I'd be happy with either one, since
                     A   **B**

both of wines seem excellent and no guest seems to be complaining.
       C   **D**

UNIT

23 Past Time Frame

Using Adverbs and Aspect to Indicate Time Relationships

EXERCISE 1   (*Focus 2*)

What is the time relationship between the highlighted verbs in each of the numbered sentences? How is the time relationship indicated: By sequence? By adverbials? By aspect? By both? The first sentence has been done for you as an example.

1. By the time Janice **got** home, the ice cream **had melted** in the car.

   First action: _had melted_

   Second action: _got home_

   How indicated: _aspect and adverbial (by the time that)_

2. Janice **had been waiting** in traffic when her car phone **rang.**

   First action: _____

   Second action: _____

   How indicated: _____

3. Janice **returned** to her desk and **picked up** her messages.

   First action: _____

   Second action: _____

   How indicated: _____

4. Janice **didn't pay** her rent on Thursday because her paycheck **had not been deposited.**

   First action: _____

   Second action: _____

   How indicated: _____

5. The water **had been boiling** for several minutes before Tom **turned** the heat **down.**

   First action: _____

   Second action: _____

   How indicated: _____

6. The mayor **signed** the papers and **ended** the meeting.

First action: _____

Second action: _____

How indicated: _____

EXERCISE 2 (Focus 3)

Read each sentence and select the answer (a or b) that correctly expresses the implied meaning.

1. Carol turned on the news while she was making dinner.
   a. Carol was watching television and then she started to make dinner.
   b. Carol was making dinner and she also watched television.

2. The two police officers were standing in front of the bank when I went in.
   a. The police officers were already there.
   b. The police officers arrived after I entered the bank.

3. While I was paying for my purchases, Sandra was still looking at clothes.
   a. Sandra had been looking at clothes for a while.
   b. Sandra only started to look at clothes when I went to pay for my purchases.

4. When the hurricane passed by the house, all of the windows broke.
   a. The windows were already broken at the time the hurricane passed by.
   b. The windows broke as a result of the hurricane.

5. The cat was sleeping peacefully when the owner decided to pet it.
   a. The cat was sleeping and then the owner petted it.
   b. The cat fell asleep because the owner was petting it.

EXERCISE 3 (Focus 4)

Choose the appropriate form of each verb in parentheses in the passage below. There may be more than one correct choice. Discuss your answers with a partner.

(1) During the last few months of my two-year research trip to Italy, I (constantly looked/was constantly looking) in old bookstores. **(2)** I (was trying/tried) to find all of the research material that I would need before I (was returning/returned) home. **(3)** During the last month, I (was going/went) into one bookstore so many times that I got to know the owner. **(4)** Soon we (had/were having) coffee every day.

(5) As I (was looking/looked) through his files, I (was finding/found) the name of the exact book I (was needing/needed). **(6)** He (helped/was helping) me find the book the day before I (was leaving/left).

Use the past perfect in the following sentences only if it is necessary to the meaning of the sentence. Otherwise use the simple past or past progressive.

1. Charles _____ (go) to talk to his advisor about the classes he _____ (register) for the week before.

2. The hurricane _____ (destroy) so many buildings that the town was declared a disaster area.

3. I _____ (look) everywhere for my keys when Jack _____ (find) them.

4. When Ted _____ (hear) that he _____ (was drafted), he _____ (call) his parents long distance.

5. As soon as Bill got home, he _____ (notice) that the dog _____ (chew) his shoes.

6. Carol _____ (be) upset about paying her rent since she _____ (not get) any paychecks for two months.

EXERCISE 5   *(Focus 5)*

Decide whether the past perfect or the past perfect progressive is the appropriate tense for the verbs in parentheses.

1. Catherine _____ (search) for an excuse not to go to the party even before she noticed the flat tire.

2. I _____ (finish) my project, so I was able to go to the lake.

3. It _____ (rain) for three days when the bridge collapsed.

4. Marilyn was upset because so many of her relatives _____ (use) her pool all summer.

5. By the first week of the semester, Toshi _____ (get) all the classes he wanted.

6. In October, Larry finally received the check that he _____ (wait) for since August.

Decide whether the verbs below should be in the past tense, past perfect, or past perfect progressive. More than one answer may be correct. Discuss your answers with a partner.

1. Christopher Columbus _____ (try) to find a new route to India when he _____ (discover) islands near what is now the United States.

2. I _____ (be [negative]) satisfied with the way my car _____ (run), so I _____ (take) it to the mechanic.

3. Paul _____ (write) several letters to the company before he _____ (decide) to call and speak directly to the manager.

4. Eric _____ (train) for the swimming competition for months before he found out that he was selected for the team.

5. When I _____ (get) to the supermarket, I realized that I _____ (leave) my wallet at home.

6. Professor Zardoff _____ (spend) a great deal of time in the lab before the project was completed.

7. Jack _____ (go) back to the store and _____ (exchange) the item.

8. Christine _____ (listen) to their conversation for quite some time before they _____ (realize) it.

UNIT

24 Modals in Past Time

EXERCISE 1 (Focus 1)

Decide whether the following sentences are (a) requests or (b) questions about your past habits or abilities.

EXAMPLE: Would you play doctor when you were a child? **(b)**

1. Could you tell me where the admissions office is?

2. Do you think that you could park the car without hitting the curb?

3. Could you write your name when you were four years old?

4. Would you mind not smoking?

5. Would you act as if you were older when you were in high school?

6. Could you drive when you lived in your country?

EXERCISE 2 (Focus 2)

Complete the puzzle by writing the answers in the blanks. The first one has been done for you.

1. You are supposed to _____ after a performance.
2. Eve was not allowed to eat this.
3. I was supposed to _____ the floor before I waxed it.
4. Catherine was allowed to _____ up late on weekends.
5. Students are not allowed to _____ gum in pronunciation class.
6. In his country, Mahtobe had to _____ up when the teacher entered the room.
7. You are not supposed to serve corn on the _____ at a very formal dinner party.
8. "Would you _____ not smoking?"
9. You are supposed to _____ your term papers.
10. Many children are not allowed to _____ the phone.

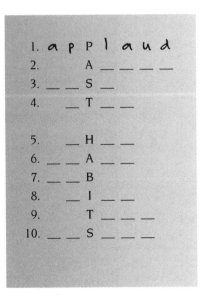

```
1. a p P l a u d
2.      A _ _ _ _
3. _ _ S _
4.    _ T _ _ _
5.    _ H _ _ _
6. _ _ A _ _ _
7. _ _ B
8.    _ I _ _ _
9.    T _ _ _ _
10. _ _ S _ _ _
```

Write four statements about things that you *were allowed to do* during summer vacation. Write four statements about things that you *were not allowed to do* when you were studying during the semester.

ALLOWED:

1. _____

   _____

2. _____

   _____

3. _____

   _____

4. _____

   _____

NOT ALLOWED:

1. _____

   _____

2. _____

   _____

3. _____

   _____

4. _____

   _____

EXERCISE 4   (Focus 2)

Write four statements about what you had to do to get a visa to come to the United States.

HAD TO:

1. _____

_____

2. _____

_____

3. _____

_____

4. _____

_____

EXERCISE 5   (Focus 2)

Rewrite your partner's answers to Exercise 4.

EXAMPLE: I had to stand in line at the American Embassy.

When Toshi wanted to get an F-1 visa, he had to stand in line at the American Embassy.

1. _____

_____

2. _____

_____

3. _____

_____

4. _____

_____

Ask your partner about four things that he or she *was supposed to do* when he or she was still living at home. Report this information in the spaces below.

EXAMPLE: Eric was supposed to walk the dog every night.

1. _____

_____

2. _____

_____

3. _____

_____

4. _____

_____

EXERCISE 7 *(Focus 3)*

Decide whether the following statements refer to general ability or specific circumstances.

1. Patrick wasn't able to pick up his dry cleaning. _____

2. Jack could drive when he was younger. _____

3. I couldn't get the manager to accept my check. _____

4. Ludmilla could speak two languages. _____

5. Gary was able to do square roots in his head. _____

6. The government could change the rules. _____

Decide whether *could* or *be able to* should be used in the following sentences. Then fill in each blank with the correct form.

EXAMPLE: <u>Was he able to</u> go to France? No, he <u>couldn't / wasn't able to</u> go. But he <u>was able to</u> take a three-day vacation closer to home.

1. Patrick _____ find his passport. He _____ use it, however, since it had expired last year.

2. Mary broke her leg last month, so she _____ hike in the woods with us.

3. Mary _____ stay by the tent and mix drinks for us when we returned from our hike.

4. Jack _____ find a hotel anywhere, so he decided to return to the airport.

EXERCISE 9   (*Focus 4*)

Determine whether the verbs in the following passage are best expressed with either *would* or *used to*. In some cases more than one answer is acceptable.

DUANE GILLOGLY

    (1) When I was a child, my family _____ (visit) my grandfather's farm. **(2)** My grandfather _____ (live) in the country. **(3)** He _____ (raise) cattle for beef. **(4)** I _____ (feed) the cows every morning. **(5)** The cows roamed over many miles because the farm _____ (be) quite large. **(6)** My grandfather _____ (let) me ride on the back of one of the cows in the evening. **(7)** I _____ (be) able to visit the farm as an adult, but not anymore. **(8)** My grandfather sold it last year.

Underline all the modal structures that refer to future events or intentions in these passages.

1. **(A)** Although Perry wasn't to open his own business for another ten years, he took accounting classes in his spare time. **(B)** He would work for three other bosses before he saved enough money to open his store. **(C)** Perry was definitely going to be prepared for the future.

2. **(A)** When James was in the army, he used to dream about his future vacations. **(B)** James would write up travel plans for the countries that he wanted to visit. **(C)** He knew that he was eventually going to visit many of these countries. **(D)** James was to become a travel writer many years and many trips later.

EXERCISE 11 *(Focus 5)*

Decide which form, *would* or *was/were going to*, you should use in the following sentences. In some cases, either may be correct.

1. **(A)** Carol decided to transfer to another college. **(B)** She _____ major in chemistry. **(C)** First she _____ register for her new courses. **(D)** Then she _____ look for a part-time job.

2. **(A)** As soon as the results of the exam were announced, the grade list _____ be posted. **(B)** Students _____ come to see the results. **(C)** Then they _____ call each other to discuss their grades.

3. **(A)** Barbara didn't know what she _____ do about the problem. **(B)** The police told her that the thief _____ probably get a home alarm system. **(C)** Maybe she _____ move.

Decide which sentences are correct and which are incorrect and write "C" or "I" next to each sentence. For the incorrect sentences, provide the correct responses.

EXAMPLE: I would mention the chocolate stain on the side of your new skirt, but maybe I shouldn't. <u>I was going to mention...</u>

1. My doctor would postpone my surgery, so I couldn't eat after 6 P.M. last night.

_____

_____

2. Wouldn't you send me my contract? I haven't received it yet.

_____

_____

3. We weren't going to extend our lease on our apartment, but we didn't have time to look for another one.

_____

_____

4. Chuck didn't want to leave his car. It would start raining any minute.

_____

_____

UNIT

 **25** Reported Speech

EXERCISE 1 **(Focus 1)**

Change the following direct quotations to reported speech using the cues provided.

EXAMPLE: The plans are close to getting the city's approval." The architect told us that...

The architect told us that the plans were close to getting the city's approval.

1. "Your child needs to come to school on time." The teacher told me...

_____

_____

2. "He often teases the other children." She didn't like the fact that...

_____

_____

3. "The supermarket cashier dropped the eggs." Pauline was annoyed that...

_____

_____

4. "The cat needs more exercise." The veterinarian explained that...

_____

_____

170 Unit 25

Restate the following sentences as direct quotations, using "The manager said…"

EXAMPLE: She reported that costs have been going up very quickly.

The manager said, "Costs are going up very quickly."

1. She was unhappy that we would no longer have free coffee.

_____

_____

2. She didn't like the fact that there would be no more doughnuts at staff meetings.

_____

_____

3. She was concerned that Mr. Pearson hadn't gotten any new contracts last month.

_____

_____

4. She was concerned that two employees had left for other jobs.

_____

_____

_____

EXERCISE 3   *(Focus 2)*

Change the following sentences to reported speech using the verbs in parentheses.

EXAMPLE: The coach said, "You guys will have to work harder." (insist)

The coach insisted that the team members would have to work harder.

1. The teacher said, "Bill will probably need extra tutoring." (commented)

_____

_____

2. The bus driver said, "I could have avoided the accident." (admitted)

_____

_____

3. Jack's doctor said, "Your father shouldn't continue smoking." (stated)

_____

_____

4. Patrick said, "The reports are ready to be sent." (mentioned)

_____

_____

5. The government official said, "The new tax rates will be released tomorrow." (announced)

_____

_____

EXERCISE 4   (*Focus 3*)

Change the following direct quotations into reported speech.

EXAMPLE: Jack said, "My students have to write a ten-page term paper."

Jack said that his students have to write a ten-page term paper.

1. Jack said, "My wife and your husband have a lot in common."

_____

_____

2. Jack's wife said, "My husband thinks that I can read his mind."

_____

_____

3. Jack's brother said, "My brother and I often go fishing on Mary's boat."

_____

_____

4. Jack's mother said, "Jack needs to visit me more often."

_____

_____

EXERCISE 5   (*Focus 4*)

Change the following statements into reported speech.

EXAMPLE: Cecelia said, "I came onto campus to see my advisor, but he won't be back until tomorrow."

Cecelia said that she had come onto campus to see her advisor, but he won't be back until the next day.

1. Last week Mary told me, "I have already taken all of the units I need for my degree."

_____

_____

2. When Max saw his sister he promised her, "I will definitely be there for your graduation."

_____

_____

3. On Saturday evening Peter mentioned, "I can go to your concert after all."

_____

_____

4. When he stopped me, the INS agent said, "I want to see your green card and your driver's license."

_____

_____

_____

EXERCISE 6   (Focus 4)

Change the following direct quotations into reported speech.

EXAMPLE: Pat said, "I came here to register, but registration is closed until Monday."

Pat said that he had gone there to register, but registration was
closed until Monday.

1. When I saw Tomoko last week she told me, "The counselor won't be able to help me get into ESL classes until tomorrow."

_____

_____

2. Yesterday the car mechanic said, "I won't be able to get the part I need to repair your engine until two days from today."

_____

_____

3. Last week the dormitory manager said, "You will have to move all of your things out of your room by tonight. The plumbers are going to fix the pipes in the room above yours."

_____

_____

_____

4. When I went to the embassy, the official said, "These papers have to be signed and returned by tomorrow at the latest."

_____

_____

EXERCISE 7   (*Focus 5*)

Underline the reported statements in the following passage. Restate each one as a direct quotation. Be sure to make the other necessary changes of tense and reference. The first one has been done for you as an example.

EXAMPLE: _Janice's boss said, "Don't wear red nail polish."_

Janice left college for a while and started to work. **(1)** During Janice's first week on the job, her boss told her not to wear red nail polish. **(2)** Her coworker told her that they never chewed gum while sitting at the front desk. **(3)** The woman who sold coffee from the coffee cart warned her that refills were not allowed. **(4)** On Friday, her boss reminded her that she couldn't leave early. **(5)** When Janice got home that evening, her mother told her that there was no food in the refrigerator for dinner. That was it! Janice decided to return to school and the peace of her dormitory.

2. _____

_____

3. _____

_____

4. _____

_____

5. _____

_____

Bob had been seeing Maryanne after school for a few months and he wanted to take her to the movies on a Saturday night. Maryanne's father, Mr. Barbato, was very strict and he insisted on meeting Bob first. When Bob met Mr. Barbato, he had to answer quite a few questions.

Read the following story. Then write as quotations the questions that Maryanne's father asked Bob.

EXAMPLE: *"Do you have a job?"*_____

(1) Mr. Barbato wanted to know if Bob had a job. (2) He asked what Bob's grades were. (3) He asked whether or not Bob had had any speeding tickets or other problems with the law. (4) Mr. Barbato wanted to know if Bob was planning to pay for his education. (5) After fifteen or twenty such questions, Bob began to wonder if he really ever wanted to see Maryanne again.

_____

_____

_____

_____

_____

_____

EXERCISE 9   (*Focus 7*)

Rewrite the following indirect commands and requests as direct quotations.

EXAMPLE: On the first day of student orientation, Akiko was told by her counselor to get an ID card.

*The counselor told Akiko, "Get an ID card."*_____

1. Another advisor told her to get an American checking account.

_____

_____

2. Akiko's new roommate ordered her to take the bed near the window.

_____

_____

3. Akiko's host family asked her if she would like to go to the mall with them.

_____

_____

4. Her English professor warned her to type all of her assignments.

_____

_____

5. Akiko's friend asked her if she was happy in her new school.

_____

_____

EXERCISE 10 (Focus 8)

Decide whether tense changes are required for all the verb phrases in the following sentences when they are changed to reported speech. If a tense change is not required, state why.

EXAMPLES: My mother told me, "Honor has no price."

<u>No change. Timeless truth.</u>_____

Alicia's sister advised her, "Take your most difficult courses before you apply to graduate school."

<u>Alicia's sister advised her to take her most difficult courses before</u>
<u>she applied to graduate school.</u>_____

1. Marilyn said, "If I knew then what I know now, my life would be very different."

_____

_____

2. Just five minutes ago the child asked, "Are we there yet?"

_____

_____

3. Last month my roommate asked me, "Do you mind if I borrow your chemistry notes?"

_____

_____

4. Paulette told us, "Carol is still in the hospital due to complications during her surgery."

_____

_____

5. Catherine warned her roommate, "I will be up late typing my paper."

_____

_____

EXERCISE 11 (Focus 8)

Underline the examples of reported speech in the following passages.

1. Theresa called me to say that she had been nominated "Engineering Student of the Year."
   She told me that there were five finalists. She commented that she was the only woman
   of the five. This was quite an honor.

2. When I was a little child, I was very curious about whether Santa Claus was real. I told
   my mother that I knew where the North Pole was. I announced that I had written Santa
   a letter. Naturally, I wasn't surprised when I received a return letter.

3. I wonder if you know how I can reach Mr. Zoltan. Do you know whether he's still teaching
   history? I would like to tell him that I'm getting my M.A. in history.

TOEFL®

Test Preparation Exercises
Units 23–25

Choose the *one* word or phrase that best completes each sentence.

1. When Daniel disappeared and there was absolutely no trace of him, we realized that he _____ his disappearance for a long time.
    - (A) planned
    - (B) had been planning
    - (C) had planned
    - (D) was planning

2. We _____ a ten-page paper for Professor Danielson, but I said what I had to say in seven pages, so I turned it in with an explanatory note to the instructor.
    - (A) must write
    - (B) should write
    - (C) were supposed to write
    - (D) should have written

3. Georgia said that she _____ from a business trip the day before.
    - (A) was returning
    - (B) would return
    - (C) returned
    - (D) had returned

4. The weatherman predicted that the snow _____ falling sometime the following afternoon.
    - (A) will start
    - (B) would start
    - (C) was about to start
    - (D) was supposed to start

5. Jodi _____ her word, so now she had to make good on her promise.
    - (A) had given
    - (B) had been giving
    - (C) was giving
    - (D) gave

6. Amy didn't think she had a chance of winning the piano competition, but she _____ by turning in an inspired performance of Prokofiev's Third Concerto.
    - (A) could win
    - (B) could have won
    - (C) was able to win
    - (D) had won

7. When Tim asked why he had to go to bed, his mother repeated to him the saying that the early bird _____ the worm.
    - (A) was supposed to catch
    - (B) was able to catch
    - (C) caught
    - (D) catches

8. As a child, Chris wondered why _____ so much of their time complaining about or criticizing other people.
    - (A) are people spending
    - (B) people spends
    - (C) people spent
    - (D) did people spend

178   Units 23–25

9. Sonya now has a BMW, but she _____ a Volkswagen "Beetle."
    (A) would own   (C) had owned
    (B) used to own   (D) was owning

10. After he _____ up the cafe, he walked the dark streets of town until sunrise.
    (A) had closed   (C) has closed
    (B) had been closing   (D) closes

Identify the *one* underlined word or phrase that must be changed for the sentence to be grammatically correct.

11. When Cyril <u>called</u> Sandra, he <u>was</u> extremely nervous, partly because he <u>hadn't talked</u> to
            A   **B**   **C**
her in such a long time but mostly because he <u>had still been</u> in love with her.
                                          D

12. The boss stated that if the company <u>is making</u> a profit we would get a raise but that as
                               A
far as he <u>could see</u>, it <u>didn't look</u> like anything <u>was going to</u> change.
       B   **C**   **D**

13. The personnel officer wanted to know <u>whether</u> I <u>had ever supervised</u> a large project, and
                                  A   **B**
I answered that I <u>did</u>; I told him about the time I <u>directed</u> the renovation of the McKinley
             C   **D**
Building.

14. At the age of 17, Joel <u>already felt</u> ashamed of the time he <u>wasted</u>, and he <u>would dream</u> of
                    A   **B**   **C**
all the great things that he <u>would accomplish</u> in his life.
                   D

15. They <u>would cancel</u> the flight, but then the weather <u>cleared up</u> a bit and the runway
       A   **B**
conditions <u>improved</u>, so the plane <u>was able to</u> take off.
         C   **D**

16. NASA <u>calculated</u> that the average global temperature in 1990 <u>was</u> 60°F, the warmest on
      A   **B**
record, and the British Meteorological Office reported that 1990 was the warmest it
<u>has been</u> since they <u>began</u> keeping records in 1850.
 C   **D**

17. Dr. Katz called her office to say that she <u>had been working</u> on her research all night and
                                    A
that she <u>had</u> so little sleep that she <u>was feeling</u> quite sick, so she <u>would not be coming</u>
        B   **C**   **D**
into the clinic that morning.

18. Andrew was panic-stricken that he <u>was going to</u> miss an important meeting because his
                                          A

alarm clock <u>had not rung</u> when it <u>was supposed to</u> and his car wouldn't start, so he
            B   **C**

<u>must have caught</u> a cab to work.
      D

19. Nick <u>was not really thinking</u> much about the priorities in his life until he <u>got</u> seriously ill,
             A   **B**

and then he realized <u>what was</u> really important to him and <u>what he should do</u> with the
                       C   **D**

rest of his life.

20. With time for reflection while in the hospital, Nick decided that he <u>should</u>

<u>definitely spend</u> more time with his family and best friends, that he <u>might visit</u> the places
      A   **B**

he had always wanted to see, and most definitely that he <u>must</u> finally finish reading
                                                           C

Proust's novel when he <u>felt</u> better.
                        D